LIFT ME UP TO YOUR LIGHT, LORD

LIFT ME UP TO YOUR LIGHT, LORD

FINDING GOD'S BLESSINGS IN THE MIDST OF OUR TRIALS

ARIANNE FINAN

XULON PRESS

Xulon Press
2301 Lucien Way #415
Maitland, FL 32751
407.339.4217
www.xulonpress.com

Unless otherwise indicated, Scripture quotations taken from the Holy Bible,
New International Version (NIV). Copyright © 1973, 1978, 1984, 2011 by
Biblica, Inc.™. Used by permission. All rights reserved.

ISBN-13: 978-1-6628-0828-9
Ebook: 978-1-6628-0829-6

To my mother, Patty.

In thirteen short years, you taught me how to love deeply, care greatly, and give generously. You are missed dearly!

February 13, 1952–September 26, 1997

CONTENTS

"The one who sowed the good seed is the Son of Man.
The field is the world,
and the good seed stands for the people of the kingdom."

Matthew 13:37-38

ACKNOWLEDGMENTS

A Special Thank You To...

God Almighty and His Son, Jesus Christ- For being my guiding light through my trials and helping to transform me into the person You created me to be.

My husband- For encouraging me to keep writing this book. During health challenges, big life decisions, and a move across the U.S., you stood by my side and were so supportive.

My precious daughter- Your smile brings me joy every day. From a young age, you have shown how caring you are, from reading your books to me while we were at doctors' appointments to giving me big hugs and kisses. I am so proud of you for the sweet girl you are.

My family, especially my main three:

Dad- For stepping up and taking on dual roles when mom died. Although there were difficult moments, you provided a loving and caring home for Alissa and me and helped give us opportunities to be successful in life.

Gram- Your strength, love and cheerful spirit has always been an inspiration to me. I have always appreciated the way you have given a listening ear and have inspired me to find answers in my healing journey.

Alissa- You have been more to me than a sister. . . you have been my best friend. I am thankful for our close bond and the way our children have become the best of friends.

My spiritual family and friends, especially:

Pastor Dan- For your incredible encouragement and guidance. Thank you for reviewing the Bible stories and verses in my book.

Hannah and Sarah- For taking time out of your busy schedules to read through my manuscript and provide thoughtful insights. I am grateful for your friendship.

INTRODUCTION

I needed answers.

How could I find healing?

As I was circled around with other Christian women at my church discussing a Bible study, these words from James jumped off the page:

"Do not merely listen to the word, and so deceive yourselves. DO WHAT IT SAYS" (James 1:22).

God gave me the answer I needed. He made it clear to me. I needed to start following His commands rather than just listening to them.

Before that moment I had been trying to navigate through life on my own. I had endured hardships and trials, and now I was facing health issues. At a young age, my aunt and mom had passed away from cancer within two years of each other. This time during my teenage life was incredibly significant. I had to accept the fact that I would not have my mother's advice and expertise on friendships, boys, and what dress to wear for prom. My mother would not be present to watch me walk down the aisle at my wedding. And after receiving a diagnosis of polycystic ovarian syndrome (PCOS) after several failed attempts to get pregnant, I would not have my mother's shoulder to cry on.

In my journey I started to research, and I began to rely on the help of doctors to determine what medications and techniques could bring healing to my body. And just when I thought I was on the right track, I came up empty-handed. Or so I thought. Instead God was directing my eyes to Him. He taught me this lesson: my knowledge and the knowledge of others could help me a little bit, but the power of God could and would transform me, heal me, and strengthen me forever.

From the moment I saw the words on the page say "Do What It Says," I began to pore over my Bible searching for God's answers. I was surprised by what I found, and I kept diving in for more. God started to lay out these steps in front of me at uniquely different points in my own healing journey. I began to follow each step, and with each step, I began to learn of another. Rather than just listening to God's words, I began to put them into practice in my own life. I began seeing transformation.

It was in the fall of 2019, when I was finishing up the final chapters of this book, that God helped me to see how all of these chapters would come together. At three in the morning, I was woken up from discomfort in my throat. The day before I had been seen by the ER after getting a small piece of food stuck in my throat. Thankfully the X-ray did not reveal anything, but my throat was still inflamed. Since I could not sleep, I walked out to the couch and sat there. The ideas of my book were circling through my mind, as I had been spending just about every day typing, revising, and praying over it. I wondered, *Why am I going through this now?* But without this circumstance, I would have missed the next twenty minutes I had with God. God brought my attention to Him, and I knew the image He had revealed to me was important. So after grabbing a piece of white paper, I etched the image on the paper.

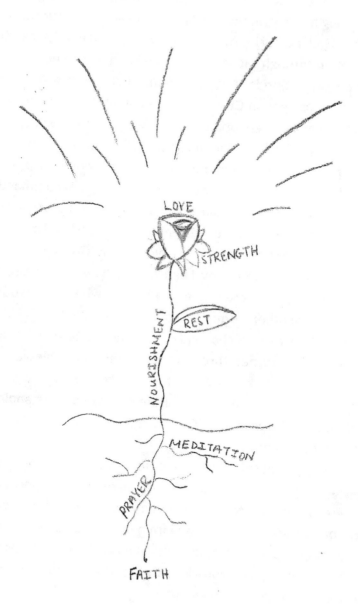

Flower growing up to God's light

After looking over this image, I understood what God was showing me. My journey had been similar to the journey of a growing plant. My journey had taken time and needed careful attention through the years. My seed had just faced big and little storms, floods, and other difficult challenges. But with planting my seed in God's soil, I was building upon my faith with prayer and meditation. I saw how my roots began to grow and emerge. And as I continued to look up to God, I learned how proper nourishment, rest, and strength would help keep me strong during my challenges. By following His commands, I was able to stand up against the storms of life and persevere through them. I could see the beautiful creation I had become in God, and with a new perspective, I found God's pure love, which gave me so much joy. I had learned how to take care of myself through my trials, and I had found what tools would help me face other storms if I would so need them.

In the next seven chapters, I will share more of my story of being transformed through God's light. The Bible verses chosen in this book specifically have spoken to me and have helped me through my own trials. In my own understanding and through the wisdom of God, I have explained what I have learned from Him.

Now, I am not sure what illness, health concern, or trial you may be facing right now, but you may be reading this because you are facing a trial that is bigger than you can handle on your own or you are interested in learning more about what the Bible says about overcoming trials. I am glad you have chosen to allow God to guide you along this journey, and I hope my story brings you encouragement.

Before you begin, I feel it is important to say this:

Finding healing from one's own illness or trial may or may not mean physical healing. That is up to God. But one may experience a deeper healing in his or her own journey. God is a God of miracles. God is capable of healing us physically (many examples in the Bible show us how this is true). The healing that God wants us to experience may be different from what we have in mind. Everyone will have a different story. Everyone will have a different healing journey. But we all have a choice to grow closer to God, and through our closeness, we can experience His light. His bright and glorious *light*. We can find healing inside of us through God.

I hope this book finds you at just the right time in your own journey. If you would like additional help in growing closer to God during your trial, then please use the prayers, questions, and Bible verses for a seven-week Bible study. I have called this the Power of Seven Challenge, and each chapter's Bible study can be completed over seven days. The Bible study is designed to help you grow closer to God and help you think of what impact you can have over your own trial and suffering.

As you continue on through the chapters of this book, please know this as you face a trial, difficult circumstance, or any other challenge:

- You are not alone.
- God is ready to teach you about His ways.
- Direct your eyes to God, and He will lead you to His light.

1

FAITH

"But I will restore you to health and heal your wounds."

Jeremiah 30:17

When I look back to when I was eleven years old, I can still remember the moment when my mom shared the news with me that her sister passed away from breast cancer. I had just walked in from school that afternoon, and after hearing those heartbreaking words, I retreated to my room and sat. I sat with God...talking to Him and praying for comfort.

Two years later I faced harder news when the teacher in my study hall class asked me one morning to gather all of my belongings and meet my dad in the front office to pick me up early from school. I already knew why, but I did not want to face the fact that my mom would no longer be with us. Her battle with ovarian cancer was over. Her suffering had finally ended. And again, after hearing the news, I retreated to my room, where I sat in disbelief. I sat with God, asking Him why and how this could happen.

With each of these experiences, I grew up seeing how suffering was a part of life. A very difficult one, at that.

But I also grew up knowing God was there for me. He was my rock in the midst of all this turmoil. At a young age, my faith was developing and growing through these difficult times. Thanks to my mom and my dad, I had learned of God through the different religious backgrounds I was exposed to. As I grew older, I began to find out who I was in my own faith, and my relationship with God grew stronger.

For Christmas in 2003, my dad gave me my first Bible. Just inside the front cover, he inscribed the message: *"May you find God's love and guidance in every aspect of your life."*

God's love I would need, and His guidance I would need even more as I began to suffer through my own health challenges after college.

During this next season in my life, I would need to rely greatly on my faith in God.

After many years of not knowing and understanding why I was experiencing abnormal symptoms, I asked several doctors to run additional labs on me. Finally I received an answer, and my doctor diagnosed me with polycystic ovarian syndrome (PCOS). At that moment I felt hopeless and discouraged. My husband and I were ready to start a family, and this diagnosis felt like it was taking away my hope of becoming a mother. As I came to God for answers, He began to point me to the Bible, showing me that I could experience healing while putting my faith and hope in Him.

One of the first stories in the Bible to give me encouragement was about a woman who had been subject to bleeding for *twelve years*. She had suffered a great deal under the care of many doctors and had spent all she had, yet instead of getting better she grew worse (Mark 5:25–26). After reading this, I could relate. For the last seven years, I had suffered through many complications from PCOS. I had seen many doctors, been through many tests, and tried many treatments, even one that caused greater harm than good in my case.

The woman in Mark thought if she could just get close enough to Jesus, she would be healed. When she did, she felt in her body that she was free from her suffering (Mark 5:29). When this happened, Jesus asked, "Who touched my clothes?" Jesus knew the power left Him (Mark 5:30). The woman finally came forward, fell to His feet, and told Him the truth. Then Jesus said to her, "Daughter, your faith has healed you. Go in peace and be freed from your suffering" (Mark 5:34).

When I read that last verse, I felt as if those words had a greater meaning. I sat for a moment and thought, *Could Jesus speak these words to me? Could these words be true for me?*

It seemed too easy. With one touch this woman's suffering was lifted away because of her faith. I knew I could not sit back any longer and do nothing. God was showing me something through this story, and I was ready to find out what. I wanted to have faith like hers. I wanted to have hope like hers. I wanted to experience the healing powers of God. But how could I do that? I needed to have a greater understanding of what faith was and how I could strengthen my faith in God. I had developed my relationship with God at a young age, but now I needed to build upon that foundation of faith. In seeing the image of the flower growing up to God's light, I could see how each of us were spread out across the earth like seeds, and I knew God had given each of us a choice to sprout our roots in Him.

I took my first step in my healing journey when I found out what it meant to have faith in the one, true God. Faith defined in the Bible is: "Confidence in what we hope for and assurance about what we do not see. This is what the ancients were commended for. By faith we understand that the universe was formed at God's command, so that what is seen was not made out of what was visible" (Heb. 11:1–3).

In the verses following this scripture in Hebrews, several examples are listed of believers who trusted God even when they could not see God's plan. They followed God's commands and obeyed His instructions. They showed exceptional faith.

For my faith to grow and not just stay a tiny seed, I would need to know more about God and understand how He is the Father; the Son; and the Holy Spirit. As I looked through scripture, I learned more about the meaning of faith. I learned it was important to understand the role of the Father, Son, and Holy Spirit in my life.

Faith in God the Father

To have faith, I believe God is who He says He is. God is the creator of the world and I believe the universe was formed at His command. If you open up your Bible to the very first book and read the very first verse, it says, "In the beginning God created the heavens and the earth" (Gen. 1:1).

As a believer, I accept this to be true, and I have faith even when I cannot see or understand how God's creation came to be.

In chapter 1 of Genesis, the writer tells us how God brought a wonderful light into the world, and how He filled the world with wonderful things, including men and women. God shows us He is our Father. He made us: "Yet you, LORD, are our Father.

We are the clay, you are the potter; we are all the work of your hand" (Isa. 64:8).

Our world was made into an incredible place. God brought life to earth, and He set Adam and Eve on earth as the first two human beings. Everything was *so good*.

But if everything was so good from the beginning, how is it that we can be faced with diseases, hardships, and suffering? How did sin enter the world? The story of Adam and Eve helps us to understand how we can face trials, and how we can become better people as we navigate through them.

God instructed Adam and Eve to follow His commands and rules. God's first instruction to them was to not eat from the tree of knowledge of good and evil. If they ate from this tree, they would die. Adam and Eve accepted this rule from God and began to follow it. However, we learn in this story that a serpent came along and fooled Eve into believing it was okay to eat from the tree: "You will not certainly die," the serpent said to the woman. "For God knows that when you eat from it your eyes will be opened, and you will be like God, knowing good and evil" (Gen. 3:4–5). Eve then picked from the tree. Eve shared the fruit with her husband, and they both ate it. Immediately, sin entered the world. God became angry, and He forced them to leave the Garden of Eden.

We may think the story ends there, but it does not. Despite what happened that day in the Garden of Eden, God still loved the world He made. God loved His people, and He could not leave the world as it was.

Over the next generations from Adam to Noah, God was saddened by how corrupt the earth had become in sin:

> The LORD saw how great the wickedness of the human race had become on the earth, and that

every inclination of the thoughts of the human heart was only evil all the time. The LORD regretted that he had made human beings on the earth, and his heart was deeply troubled. So the LORD said, "I will wipe from the face of the earth the human race I have created—and with them the animals, the birds and the creatures that move along the ground—for I regret that I have made them." But Noah found favor in the eyes of the LORD. (Gen. 6:5–8)

Reread the last sentence of those verses. Noah found favor in the eyes of the Lord. God was pleased with Noah, and He saw how Noah was faithful. God would now ask Noah to follow His commands and give him a calling.

Would Noah accept God's challenge and calling? As we read more in Genesis, we learn of how Noah, being a man of great faith, would continue to be obedient to God and follow His ways. Noah would be ready to save his family and the many animals around him from a great flood.

Now, when our world is threatened with disease or a trial comes knocking at our door, we want to believe that we have found favor in God's eyes. In showing God our faith in Him, we are showing Him we trust Him and we are willing to obey Him. We want to and need to be ready for the many challenges we may face in our lives.

Our faith must be the foundation. Is your foundation built on faith? When our house is built on God's rock, we have a strong foundation of faith. When we experience a trial of any kind, our house will not be shaken.

These verses in Luke chapter 6 help to explain how we can have a foundation built upon God's rock:

Why do you call me, "Lord, Lord," and do not do what I say? As for everyone who comes to me and hears my words and puts them into practice, I will show you what they are like. They are like a man building a house, who dug down deep and laid the foundation on rock. When a flood came, the torrent struck that house but could not shake it, because it was well built. But the one who hears my words and does not put them into practice is like a man who built a house on the ground without a foundation. The moment the torrent struck that house, it collapsed and its destruction was complete. (Luke 6:46–49)

The men and women who listen to God and choose to put Him first are building a strong foundation of faith. If you are choosing to ignore God's words and navigate through life on your own, then you are building a foundation that can drift away quickly like sand. Jesus is saying that when a flood comes, the ones who have built their houses on a strong foundation of faith will not be affected by the flood's destruction. When I lost my mother, when I was diagnosed with PCOS, and when I dealt with infertility, I came up stronger as I dealt with each of these trials because my trust is in God and I have chosen to build my foundation upon God's rock.

Noah is a great example of one who built a foundation of faith in God. God asked him to build a 450-foot-long ark, and "Noah did everything just as God commanded him" (Gen. 6:22). Noah had never built a boat like this before, but he trusted God. He followed every instruction he was given, and God protected him. God kept his whole family safe during the flood, as well as all the animals he had been asked to bring on the ark with him.

After hearing the story of Noah, the question that still may be lingering in your mind is: Am I ready to put my full trust in God and walk with Him during this trial and the ones to come?

We are taking a step to deepen our faith. There is no greater time than right now. I know I could not survive life on my own, especially not when I know there is suffering going on all around the world and I could face a bigger trial tomorrow.

As I am calling on God, as my Father, I am believing He is by my side. I see how He stood by Noah during the flood and watched over his family. My faith allows me to believe that He will protect me as well during my trials. When I have called on God, He has been there for me, and I believe He will stand by you as well. As you read this next verse, can you feel the protection God provides and see how God's focus is on the people He loves?

"The LORD himself goes before you and will be with you; he will never leave you nor forsake you. Do not be afraid; do not be discouraged" (Deut. 31:8).

Faith in God the Son (Jesus Christ)

Many generations had passed between when Noah walked the earth and when God would send His one and only Son. God had been waiting for the perfect moment to unveil His *great* plan.

In Malachi 4:1–2 it reads, "Surely the day is coming; it will burn like a furnace. All the arrogant and every evildoer will be stubble, and the day that is coming will set them on fire," says the LORD Almighty. "Not a root or a branch will be left to them. But for you who revere my name, the sun of righteousness will rise with healing in its rays. And you will go out and frolic like well-fed calves."

At the very end of the Old Testament, we finally learn of the Son that God would send to save us all. The passage that stands out to me from these verses is, "[Those] who revere my name, the sun of righteousness will rise with healing in its rays." As I think about this verse, I see how Jesus Christ was sent to us to bring light into our lives. If I picture a sunrise in my mind, I see a great light appearing to all the world, just as Jesus Christ appears to all of us. And those who "revere" His name and who call on Him will experience His light and will be saved from all the pain, darkness, and trials in this world. Through these verses I understand that Jesus was appointed by God to bring healing to the lives who need it, and as we receive it, we will leap like calves in excitement and admiration.

God gives us the chance to be saved...to be saved from our sins and to be freed from the darkness of the world. God sent Jesus Christ to be our *light*.

What does this mean for you? What does this mean for me?

God sent His Son for us so that we may have eternal life. In John 3:16 it says, "For God so loved the world that he gave his one and only Son, that whoever believes in him shall not perish but have eternal life."

God sent His one and only Son to take away our sins. We can have eternal life when we believe in God and Jesus. How can we experience this gift?

"For it is by grace you have been saved, through faith—and this is not from yourselves, it is the gift of God—not by works, so that no one can boast" (Eph. 2:8–9).

God gives us the gift of salvation when we have faith and believe in Him. God freely gives us this gift. It is through God's grace. It is up to us to accept it or not. What this verse says is that our faith is not measured by the good we do in the world, but what is important is who we put our faith and trust in. Look at Romans 10, verses 9 and 13: "If you declare with your mouth, 'Jesus is Lord,' and believe in your heart that God raised him from the dead, you will be saved" (v. 9). For, "Everyone who calls on the name of the Lord will be saved" (v. 13).

When I call on the name of the Lord and look at how God sent Jesus Christ to earth for us, I can see the love He has for us, and I am thankful to be one of His children: "So in Christ Jesus you are all children of God through faith, for all of you who were baptized into Christ have clothed yourselves with Christ" (Gal. 3:26–27).

Read this verse again. Take it in. We are the sons of God. We are the daughters of God. We are His children. *I am a child of God*: "For he chose us in him before the creation of the world to be holy and blameless in his sight. In love he predestined us for adoption to sonship through Jesus Christ, in accordance with his pleasure and will—to the praise of his glorious grace, which he has freely given us in the One he loves" (Eph. 1:4–6).

If you have stepped away from God because of the troubles in your life or if you have never heard these words before, God sees you. If you are struggling through your trial, God sees you. If you are afraid, God sees you. Let us all call upon God and Jesus and see how much we are loved by Them.

In Luke chapter 15, we learn of a story about a young son who asked for his share of his father's estate. The young son set off to a distant country and "squandered his wealth in wild living" (Luke 15:13). The young son was starving and finally came to his senses. The young son thought to himself, "I will set out and go back to my father and say to him: 'Father, I have sinned against heaven and against you. I am no longer worthy

to be called your son; make me like one of your hired servants'"
(Luke 15:18–19).

Now, what do you think the father did when his young son
came home? Did he turn his back on him?

No.

We learn from this story that the father saw his son and
ran to him, hugging and kissing him. The father was filled
with compassion and celebrated the return of his son. The
son repented, and the father forgave him. Do you know that
God (and all of heaven) celebrates when we return to Him and
seek His forgiveness?

God does not want us to go through this trial alone. God
does not want our sin to keep us away from Him. Many of us
have sinned in one way or another. The good news is that God
does not keep a record of our wrongs (Rom. 4:8). God teaches
us about faith and His faithfulness through our sin:

> God is light; in him there is no darkness at all. If
> we claim to have fellowship with him yet walk
> in the darkness, we lie and do not live out the
> truth. But if we walk in the light, as he is in the
> light, we have fellowship with one another, and
> the blood of Jesus, his Son, purifies us from all
> sin. If we claim to be without sin, we deceive
> ourselves and the truth is not in us. If we con-
> fess our sins, he is faithful and just and will
> forgive us our sins and purify us from all unrigh-
> teousness. (1 John 1:5–9)

We cannot claim to be without sin. All of us at one time or
another will be tempted by sin. God knows this and asks us to
master it: "But if you do not do what is right, sin is crouching

at your door; it desires to have you, but you must rule over it" (Gen. 4:7).

Throughout my journey God has helped me to see my sin. When I have recognized it, asked for forgiveness, and stopped the cycle of repeating that sin, I have grown closer to God. If I live by God's truth and am purified from any unrighteousness that is holding me back, then I can break away from my old self and become a new being: "Therefore, if anyone is in Christ, the new creation has come: The old has gone, the new is here!" (2 Cor. 5:17).

When I think about the stages of a seed and the first step it needs to take to become a plant, I recognize the similarities to myself in becoming a new creation. I planted my seed, and through my faith, I have opened my life to trust God, and in doing so, my seed is ready to take this next step too. It is ready to become a new creation and sprout. As I look forward instead of behind me, I am believing God is walking next to me. God is my Father. I am His daughter, and I know He will never leave me. I take this step, and I look forward to allowing God to transform me.

In the next chapters, we will continue to discuss how we can break free from our old self and our sins and continue to walk in the light of God. But before we do, let us learn more about the life of Jesus and why God sent Him to us.

In having a relationship with God, we are also invited to have a relationship with Jesus. Jesus was sent to be an example for us. In learning about Jesus, we see that He lived a faithful life. His life was full of purpose and great accomplishments in His short lifetime. But Jesus also faced many difficult trials, and when He suffered on the cross, He trusted in the fact that God would remain faithful.

Despite the journey that Jesus had, God used Jesus to show His promise to us (that we are saved). God raised Jesus from the dead. Jesus was able to overcome death, and we are able to overcome our trials. We can relate to Jesus through our own suffering, and we can understand why God sent Jesus to be human like us:

> Since the children have flesh and blood, he too shared in their humanity so that by his death he might break the power of him who holds the power of death—that is, the devil— and free those who all their lives were held in slavery by their fear of death. For surely it is not angels he helps, but Abraham's descendants. For this reason he had to be made like them, fully human in every way, in order that he might become a merciful and faithful high priest in service to God, and that he might make atonement for the sins of the people. Because he himself suffered when he was tempted, he is able to help those who are being tempted. (Heb. 2:14–18)

This is very powerful. Jesus is human, just like us. He suffered during His lifetime and teaches us so much. What can we learn from the life of Jesus that will help us through our suffering? Jesus gives us hope that we can heal from our suffering just like the woman in Luke chapter 8. As we reach out to Him, may we also feel His touch, may we also feel His healing power.

If you take a look back over Jesus's life, you'll see all of His great accomplishments, but the one that happens over and over during the New Testament is how He healed others from their various illnesses: "Jesus went throughout Galilee, teaching in their synagogues, proclaiming the good news of the kingdom, and healing every disease and sickness among the people. News about him spread all over Syria, and people brought to him all who were ill with various diseases, those suffering severe pain, the demon-possessed, those having seizures, and the paralyzed; and he healed them" (Matt. 4:23–24).

Jesus did not heal only one type of illness, but He healed many kinds of illnesses. Jesus devoted His time and energy to healing the diseases of many:

> When Jesus came into Peter's house, he saw Peter's mother-in-law lying in bed with a fever. He touched her hand and the fever left her, and she got up and began to wait on him. When evening came, many who were demon-possessed were brought to him, and he drove out the spirits with a word and healed all the sick. This was to fulfill what was spoken through the prophet Isaiah: "He took up our infirmities and bore our diseases." (Matt. 8:14–17)

When we have faith, we believe God and Jesus will help us through our trial. We have hope in the Father and the Son. The stories in the Bible give us hope. Open up your Bible to Matthew, Mark, Luke, or John. As you scroll through these books of the Bible, what do you see? Do you see the stories over and over again of how Jesus healed many? What hope this gives me as I read through these miracles of healing! I believe if it is God's will, He will take up my infirmities and carry away my disease.

In another story in the Bible, a Canaanite woman (a gentile woman, non-Jewish) believed in Jesus's healing powers. The woman's daughter was suffering from demon possession, and she came crying to Jesus for help. The woman knelt before Jesus, and Jesus saw her heart. Jesus answered, "Woman, you have great faith! Your request is granted" (Matt. 15:28).

What if Jesus came before you and asked you if you believed He could take away your illness right now? What would you say?

In the Bible we read of another story, in which two blind men run up to Jesus and ask for His healing. Jesus asks them this very question: "Do you believe that I am able to do this?"

The men reply, "Yes, Lord."

The Lord then touches their eyes and says, "According to your faith let it be done to you" (Matt. 9:27–30).

What an amazing encounter with Jesus!

In both of these stories of healing we find a common theme. The men and women who were healed by Jesus had incredible faith. These stories help us to think about how deep our own faith is and where we stand with God.

Several years ago could I have confidently said yes to Jesus's question? I wanted to believe that God could heal me, but something was holding me back. The person I was when I was first diagnosed was scared. I was trying to be in control. When your world is turned upside down at a young age, you try to control what you can around you. Childhood experiences, or any traumatic event in your life, can affect your walk with God. I internalized a lot of pain and sadness. I grew very independent and missed out on a huge part of faith. It was not until I began suffering that I realized I needed to lean on God more. I learned it was not possible to do it all, have it all put together, and control everything around me. I needed to trust that God would help guide me through the process and I would need to follow the steps of Jesus.

If my seed was going to have any success in surviving this storm, then I would need to listen to God and allow my seed to grow in God's good soil. I needed to begin to look differently at my trial and what I was walking through. I needed to see what God wanted to show me.

I learned that God wanted to see if I trusted Him. He wanted to see my faith. When I first learned I had PCOS, I could have accepted the diagnosis and done nothing about it. I could have let this diagnosis define me. I could have let this diagnosis take over my life. But instead I began to call on God more. I realized God is my rock. My hope is in Christ, who took more than enough suffering for me. Could I be healed tomorrow? Next year? Or the day I meet Jesus in heaven? It is through my faith that I trust in His timing and not mine. We learn this is true through this Bible verse: "Humble yourselves, therefore, under God's mighty hand, that he may lift you up in due time. Cast all your anxiety on him because he cares for you" (1 Pet. 5:6–7).

Our faith allows us to let go of control and to hope in Him. Today my faith has grown and continues to be strengthened. I wait for Him and know His plan is far greater than mine.

Can these miracles of healing take place today? Is it possible for you to receive a miracle from God? Through my faith in God, I say yes. Today miracles are happening all around us. God is showing us signs across the earth. You may know of someone or heard of someone who has been healed from an illness, and you know it would not have been possible without God. In my own healing journey, I experienced a healing encounter with Jesus. Later I will be sharing my story with you. But to help us understand how these miracles happen, we must go to the Bible for answers.

In the life of Jesus, the disciples and other followers were able to see miracles take place all around them. Jesus was their greatest teacher. He showed them how God gave Him the authority to heal. Before Jesus was resurrected, Jesus told His disciples they would also be able to perform miracles:

> Don't you believe that I am in the Father, and that the Father is in me? The words I say to you I do not speak on my own authority. Rather, it is the Father, living in me, who is doing his work. Believe me when I say that I am in the Father and the Father is in me; or at least believe on the evidence of the works themselves. Very truly I tell you, whoever believes in me will do the works I have been doing, and they will do even greater things than these, because I am going to the Father. (John 14:10–12)

God lives in Jesus and Jesus lives in us when we believe in Him. We are part of Jesus Christ through God, our Father. Jesus helps His followers to understand this lesson.

Jesus knew He could not do the work of God alone. He needed others to share God's message and help heal the various illnesses. Jesus called on His twelve disciples and taught them that they would be given the power to heal as well.

How could this be possible? How could His disciples have that power? God knew we would need something to guide us and encourage us after Jesus was gone. Jesus told His disciples to wait for the gift His Father promised: the Holy Spirit (Acts 1:4–5).

Faith in God the Holy Spirit (Our Counselor)

In the New Testament, Jesus tells us God will give us a counselor, and it will be with us forever. Our great counselor is the Holy Spirit, the Spirit of Truth (John 14:16). The Holy Spirit allows us to have constant communication with God during our times of joy and during our troubles: "But the Advocate, the Holy Spirit, whom the Father will send in my name, will teach you all things and will remind you of everything I have said to you. Peace I leave with you; my peace I give you. I do not give to you as the world gives. Do not let your hearts be troubled and do not be afraid" (John 14:26–27).

The Holy Spirit brings us wisdom from God. God's wisdom is a mystery that has been hidden and that God destined for our glory before time began (1 Cor. 2:7). This wisdom does not come from the world but from the Spirit of God: "What we have received is not the spirit of the world, but the Spirit who is from God, so that we may understand what God has freely given us. This is what we speak, not in words taught us by human wisdom but in words taught by the Spirit, explaining spiritual realities with Spirit-taught words" (1 Cor. 2:12–13).

We need the Holy Spirit in our lives. We must have our ears open to hear the wisdom from God, and the Holy Spirit will help us navigate through our trials. As a counselor provides sound advice, the Holy Spirit provides important instructions from God.

In Acts chapter 2, we learn how the Holy Spirit came and what this means for us. On the day of Pentecost, God's spirit was poured out to all believers. At first many could not understand what was happening and even joked that the people talking in tongues had had too much wine. But Peter stopped the jokes immediately and shared with them the wisdom of the Old Testament prophet, Joel. Peter said,

> Fellow Jews and all of you who live in Jerusalem, let me explain this to you; listen carefully to what I say. These people are not drunk, as you suppose. It's only nine in the morning! No, this is what was spoken by the prophet Joel:
>
> > "In the last days, God says,
> > I will pour out my Spirit on all people.
> > Your sons and daughters will prophesy,
> > your young men will see visions,
> > your old men will dream dreams.
> > Even on my servants, both men and women,
> > I will pour out my Spirit in those days,
> > and they will prophesy.
> > I will show wonders in the heaven above
> > and signs on the earth below,
> > blood and fire and billows of smoke.
> > The sun will be turned to darkness
> > and the moon to blood
> > before the coming of the great and glorious
> > day of the Lord.
> > And everyone who calls
> > on the name of the Lord will be saved."
> > (Acts 2:14–21)

The disciples could feel the power of God from the Holy Spirit. What is amazing is how the disciples began performing miracles and showing signs to believers. God passed His wisdom to them, and they began to share this wisdom with the world. Through their strong faith, they went out and started healing others.

In Acts chapter 3, two of the disciples brought healing to a man. This man had been crippled from birth and every day, he would beg daily at the temple gate called Beautiful. When Peter and John were about to enter this temple, the crippled man asked them for money. The disciples told him they could not give him any money, but instead they would heal him. Instantly, the man could walk (Acts 3:1–8).

People in the town were amazed and questioned the power of the disciples. Peter responded to their remarks by saying, "By faith in the name of Jesus, this man whom you see and know was made strong. It is Jesus' name and the faith that comes through him that has completely healed him, as you can all see" (Acts 3:16).

Jesus shared His faith with the disciples and the disciples shared their faith with us. What great hope we have. What hope there is for us when we are going through a difficult time, because we have God the Father, the Son, and the Holy Spirit. God wants to communicate with us and wants us to communicate back to Him. God wants to bring us out of the darkness and into His light. God uses Jesus and the Holy Spirit to do this.

Testing of Your Faith

As we deepen our faith and our seed begins to sprout, we understand that in saying yes to God, we are opening our lives to a relationship with the Father, the Son, and the Holy Spirit. Our faith is built on this strong foundation, and when temptations or tests come our way, we are ready to stand up to them. Satan tempted Adam and Eve in the Garden of Eden, and when we are at our lowest point during our trial, remember to tread carefully. God, on the other hand, does not tempt, but God will test you along your journey, as He wants you to grow into the person He designed you to be. God wants to use you through your trial, just like He used Jesus. God taught Jesus important lessons that allowed Him to equip His disciples for their journey. Then, as they went out into the towns, they were able to equip others. Now, as we begin to face our trial, we see how God is calling us and how much He needs us. We have been chosen to be part of God's mission field.

From experiencing several trials in my life, here is what I can tell you. Some of our journeys will be harder than others, and there will be occasional bumps (tests) along the way. As you grow closer to God, you may see God testing your faith along your journey with Him. These tests may not be easy. We must remember God's promise to us. We must remember the truth in the Bible. We can live with God and Jesus forever. We can have eternal life in heaven. If we believe God is using us for a bigger purpose, we will be able to see the glory of God displayed throughout our life.

Read James chapter 1, paying particular attention to these verses: "Consider it pure joy, my brothers and sisters, whenever you face trials of many kinds, because you know that the testing of your faith produces perseverance. Let perseverance finish its work so that you may be mature and complete, not lacking anything" (James 1:2–4).

Continue on...

"Blessed is the one who perseveres under trial because, having stood the test, that person will receive the crown of life that the Lord has promised to those who love him" (James 1:12).

Go on a little further...

"Don't be deceived, my dear brothers and sisters. Every good and perfect gift is from above, coming down from the Father of the heavenly lights, who does not change like shifting shadows. He chose to give us birth through the word of truth, that we might be a kind of firstfruits of all he created" (James 1:16–18).

We must believe every good and perfect gift is from above. God sends us this promise through our trial:

> Trial (Testing Your Faith) → Develops Perseverance → Makes You Mature and Complete → So You'll Receive God's Perfect Gift: The Crown of Life

God is using us for a bigger purpose through our trials. Remember God has a plan through your trial. We can see this example made clear to us through one of the stories in the Bible. During Jesus's travels, He encountered a man who was born blind from birth. His disciples asked who sinned. "'Neither this man nor his parents sinned,' said Jesus, 'but this happened so that the works of God might be displayed in him'" (John 9:3).

When we shift our focus to see through God's eyes, we look beyond false teachings. We look beyond our suffering. We look beyond our misery. We look beyond our pain. Then we can see how we can persevere through our trial. We can see how the work of God will be displayed throughout our life. And finally, we can see God's promise at the end of it.

In the story of Abraham, we learn how Abraham and Sarah remained childless up until Abraham was one hundred years old. Their life had not been easy, but God told them He would bless them with a son named Isaac. When they were tested again after Isaac was born, Abraham obeyed God. Through

Abraham's trials, he believed, he persevered, and he was made complete through the work of God:

> Against all hope, Abraham in hope believed and so became the father of many nations, just as it had been said to him, "So shall your offspring be." Without weakening in his faith, he faced the fact that his body was as good as dead—since he was about a hundred years old—and that Sarah's womb was also dead. Yet he did not waver through unbelief regarding the promise of God, but was strengthened in his faith and gave glory to God, being fully persuaded that God had power to do what he had promised. (Rom. 4:18–21)

God chose Abraham and all the other men and women in the Bible to teach us about His ways. Through these stories, we believe we have been chosen to take on this suffering. We see where life is not easy for anyone. God saw that there was evil and suffering in the world, and that is why He sent His Son for us. Jesus did not have an easy life either, but as we proceed into the other chapters, we learn from Jesus how to rejoice in our suffering and gain a purpose within our trials: "We know that suffering produces perseverance; perseverance, character; and character, hope. And hope does not put us to shame, because God's love has been poured out into our hearts through the Holy Spirit, who has been given to us" (Rom. 5:3–5).

Through our faith, we are given hope. We do not have to walk alone; we depend on God, in whom we believe. God will give us the tools necessary to overcome our troubles and help us remember He is always with us. In your journey, your suffering will help you discover qualities that you did not know you had. Instead of us saying "Why me, God?" it will help us to say "Yes, Lord, use me."

In this chapter, we have taken our first step. We have planted our seed in God's good soil. As you read over the meaning of the parable of the sower, think about what growth you want for your seed as we continue to be transformed by God:

> The seed is the word of God. Those along the path are the ones who hear, and then the devil comes and takes away the word from their hearts, so that they may not believe and be saved. Those on the rocky ground are the ones who receive the word with joy when they hear it, but they have no root. They believe for a while, but in the time of testing they fall away. The seed that fell among thorns stands for those who hear, but as they go on their way they are choked by life's worries, riches, and pleasures, and they do not mature. But the seed on good soil stands for those with a noble and good heart, who hear the word, retain it, and by persevering produce a crop. (Luke 8:11–15)

My Prayer for the Readers of This Book:

Dear God,

I pray that each reader of this book will see You right now and their faith will be made strong to know that You can bring healing into their lives. You have chosen each one of them, and as they walk in Your light, I ask that You may transform their lives to do the work You have planned for them. As they plant their seed in Your good soil, may they become a new creation. Today is a fresh start with You, and through their faith, may they believe their suffering will be used to glorify You.

Amen.

Week 1: The Power of Seven Challenge

- **Read it, ponder it, and apply it**
- **For the next seven days, focus on deepening your faith in God. On each day of the week, open your Bible to *read* the verse listed. Then *ponder* it and answer the daily question. At the end of the week, *apply* what you have learned and come up with a plan to help yourself grow closer to God.**

Day 1

- Read: Hebrews 10:19–23
- Daily Question: How is God faithful?

Day 2

- Read: Matthew 8:5–13
- Daily Question: Is your house built on a foundation of faith? How strong is your faith?

Day 3

- Read: Ephesians 4:20–24
- Daily Question: How can you become a new creation?

Day 4

- Read: John 19:16–19
- Daily Question: Think about the trials Jesus had to endure during His life. Even during His last hours before His death, Jesus was forced to carry the cross on His back. What a struggle it was to carry that heavy cross! Think about what trials you are facing right now. Do you feel like your trials are weighing you down?

Day 5

- Read: Matthew 8:1–4
- Daily Question: As you think about this sentence—"He took up our infirmities and bore our diseases"—begin to write down your trials on the cross that is provided. Whatever the amount, write all of them down and imagine giving each one to Jesus.

After you have completed this exercise, take a minute to look up the song *I Am Not Alone* by Kari Jobe.[1] Music can be healing in many ways, and God may even speak to you in this moment. As you look over the words on your cross, sit and listen to these powerful verses. How are you feeling after giving up your trial(s) to God and Jesus?

Day 6

- Read: John 5:1–15
- Daily Question: Do you believe you can find healing? Do you want to be well? Is anything holding you back from saying yes?

Day 7

- Read: Romans 5:1–5
- Daily Question: What hope can you find in your trial?

Apply It: How Can You Grow Closer to God's Light?

1. What small step can you take this week to deepen your faith?

    (Ex. Purchase a Bible)

2. What big step can you take over this year to deepen your faith?

    (Ex. Join a small group)

3. How will you carry out your plans?

    (Ex. Research which Bible is best for you; search your church website for small groups and sign up)

2

PRAYER

"Be joyful in hope, patient in affliction, faithful
in prayer."

Romans 12:12

The foundation of our faith begins with a relationship with
God the Father, the Son, and the Holy Spirit. In order
to develop a strong relationship, we need to be in constant
communication with God. At the end of the first chapter, we
learned about how we can communicate with God through the
Holy Spirit. As we take another step, we want our foundation
to grow stronger. We want our roots to develop and begin to
spread throughout the ground.

In this chapter we will learn what the Bible says about
prayer and how it can help us in our healing journey. When I
have thought about my prayer time, I have seen it as a time
when I can bring my requests to God and a time to praise God

for what He has done in my life. Over the years, my prayers have changed and have become much more meaningful. God has taught me how to communicate better with Him, and when I look to the scriptures, I can approach Him more freely.

Before we begin to pray to God, I feel it is important to understand who God is and what He is capable of. In the first chapter, we learned that God is faithful. His miracles have been shared all throughout history. And the miracle I continue to come back to is the story of how Mary became pregnant with Jesus through the Holy Spirit. God's mighty power allowed Jesus to be born into this world. And like Jesus, all of us were brought into creation. Each one of us is significant to Him, and when we face troubles, we understand that God is there for us because we are His own.

In the Bible we learn many more characteristics of God. To help us in our journey, keep in mind these three points about God: God is the God of creation, God is an all-knowing God, and God is a God of all comfort. These three characteristics of God will help us in our time of need and will give us an understanding of who He is.

God of Creation:

God uniquely designed each of us and had a plan for us before we were even born. In Psalm 139, verses 13–16 state:

> For you created my inmost being; you knit me together in my mother's womb. I praise you because I am fearfully and wonderfully made; your works are wonderful, I know that full well. My frame was not hidden from you when I was made in the secret place, when I was woven

together in the depths of the earth. Your eyes saw my unformed body; all the days ordained for me were written in your book before one of them came to be.

Do you believe you were fearfully and wonderfully made? God wants us to know that we are His precious creation.

God Is an All-Knowing God:

God knows everything about us.

"Nothing in all creation is hidden from God's sight. Everything is uncovered and laid bare before the eyes of him to whom we must give account" (Heb. 4:13).

If nothing is hidden from God, then He sees and hears all, including our words, actions, and what is in our hearts.

"You have searched me, LORD, and you know me. You know when I sit and when I rise; you perceive my thoughts from afar. You discern my going out and my lying down; you are familiar with all my ways. Before a word is on my tongue you, LORD, know it completely" (Ps. 139:1–4).

Do you believe God knows you?

God wants us to know that He sees us and He is familiar with all our ways.

God of All Comfort:

God offers us compassion during our tough times.

Praise be to the God and Father of our Lord Jesus Christ, the Father of compassion and the God of all comfort, who comforts us in all our troubles, so that we can comfort those in any trouble with the comfort we ourselves receive from God. For just as we share abundantly in the sufferings of Christ, so also our comfort abounds through Christ. If we are distressed, it is for your comfort and salvation; if we are comforted, it is for your comfort, which produces in you patient endurance of the same sufferings we suffer. And our hope for you is firm, because we know that just as you share in our sufferings, so also you share in our comfort. (2 Cor. 1:3–7)

Through the trials we suffer, we learn to rely on God and not on ourselves.

"But this happened that we might not rely on ourselves but on God, who raises the dead. He has delivered us from such a deadly peril, and he will deliver us again. On him we have set our hope that he will continue to deliver us, as you help us by your prayers" (2 Cor. 1:9–11).

Do you believe God is there for you?

God wants us to know He can lift us up above our suffering. He will comfort us during our most difficult times and rejoice with us during our most joyful times.

Can you see how significant you are to Him? It is from these verses that we learn that God knows every detail of our being and our lives. Each one of us is important to Him. He has taken the time to create us, to know us, and to be with us. When we enter into this relationship with Him during our prayer time, we need to keep in mind the many qualities of His being.

God's Qualities

A passage in the Bible that allows us to see what God encompasses can be found in the book of Ephesians. In Ephesians, Paul—an apostle of Jesus Christ—speaks to believers in Ephesus, telling them about God. As you look over these verses, read them slowly, carefully paying attention to what God can offer us.

Ephesians 1:15–23 reads:

> For this reason, ever since I heard about your faith in the Lord Jesus and your love for all God's people, I have not stopped giving thanks for you, remembering you in my prayers. I keep asking that the God of our Lord Jesus Christ, the glorious Father, may give you the Spirit of wisdom and revelation, so that you may know him better. I pray that the eyes of your heart may be enlightened in order that you may know the hope to which he has called you, the riches of his glorious inheritance in his holy people, and his incomparably great power for us who believe. That power is the same as the mighty strength he exerted when he raised Christ from the dead and seated him at his right hand in the heavenly realms, far above all rule and authority, power and dominion, and every name that is invoked, not only in the present age but also in the one to come. And God placed all things under his feet and appointed him to be head over everything for the church,

which is his body, the fullness of him who fills everything in every way.

From these verses, we see:

➢ God is a God of wisdom
➢ God is a God of hope
➢ God is a God of great power
➢ God is a God of mighty strength
➢ God is a God of fullness who fills everything in every way

When we open our lives to God, He shares His gifts with us. He teaches us how to have wisdom, hope, power, and strength. During our trial, we should not feel empty, but we should feel full. God blesses us with each of these gifts. As we go to God in prayer, remember who He is. Remember what He is capable of. God invites us to come to Him, and as we do, believe that He is standing there with open arms, ready to fill us in every way.

Let us come to God freely and share with Him the problems that we face: "In him and through faith in him we may approach God with freedom and confidence" (Eph. 3:12).

It is through our faith that we can come to God and be ourselves. We can show our true self to Him. As we think about how we can approach Him with this freedom and confidence, let us learn from Jesus and His disciples about how they prayed.

Time to Pray

There is no specific rule in the Bible that states when we should pray, but we do learn in Mark 1:35 that Jesus chose a time when He could have quality time with God: "Very early in the morning, while it was still dark, Jesus got up, left the house and went off to a solitary place, where he prayed."

When I have had quiet moments to myself in the morning or when no one is around during the day, I find this time to be the most meaningful time with God. At times I may need God when I'm on a long journey, at the grocery store waiting in a long line, or even in the kitchen when I'm trying to entertain my daughter, make dinner, and feed all our furry pets. But when I make the time for God outside of my normal routine, I am showing Him my faithfulness. I am showing Him I really need Him. I am showing Him I am relying on Him and trusting Him in my circumstances.

Jesus showed us that by getting up very early in the morning, He was putting God first. He was starting the day off with God. And I know I can do this too.

Place to Pray

Although we can pray anywhere, we see God prompting us to find a proper place to pray. Do you know that Jesus would separate Himself and sit in a quiet place to remove all distractions?

In Luke 5:15 it reads: "Yet the news about him spread all the more, so that crowds of people came to hear him and to be healed of their sicknesses. But Jesus often withdrew to lonely places and prayed."

Peter learned the importance of this from Jesus, and in Acts 10:9 it tells us that one day Peter went up to the roof to pray. When he was on the roof, it says, "he saw heaven opened" (Acts 10:11). Think about that for a moment. Imagine what that might have looked like. What a beautiful sight to see. Peter was alone, distraction-free, and God spoke to him through a vision.

If we are going to hear God and experience something incredible, we must remove ourselves from distractions. We must go to a place of solitude that allows us to put God first:

> And when you pray, do not be like the hypocrites, for they love to pray standing in the synagogues and on the street corners to be seen by others. Truly I tell you, they have received their reward in full. But when you pray, go into your room, close the door and pray to your Father, who is unseen. Then your Father, who sees what is done in secret, will reward you. And when you pray, do not keep on babbling like pagans, for they think they will be heard because of their many words. Do not be like them, for your Father knows what you need before you ask him. (Matt. 6:5–8)

I can think of two places in my house where I have had very real conversations with God. When I am alone with God, I feel that freeness to open my heart to Him. In my place, I feel safe. I do not have the noise from our television in the background. I do not have my phone next to me ringing. I do not have our cats and dogs trying to tap me for attention. I am with God, and that is what matters in that moment.

Way to Pray

In the book of Ephesians, Paul gives us more good advice about how to pray: "For this reason I kneel before the Father, from whom every family in heaven and on earth derives its name" (Eph. 3:14–15).

Why kneel?

One morning when I was struggling, I felt the need to kneel. My prayer became much more intentional, real, and powerful as I got on my knees and was as open and vulnerable as I could be. As I kneeled there with tears running down my cheeks, God began to peel away the hurt that was weighing me down. And with God I felt free.

With the last verse in your mind, I bring you to a verse where Jesus begins to pray for Himself, His disciples, and all believers before He is arrested. In John 17:1 it says, "He looked toward heaven and prayed."

Take a moment to imagine yourself on your knees looking up to heaven. In our relationships with friends and family, we communicate by looking and speaking directly to them. As we strengthen our relationship with God, let us speak freely and openly face-to-face with Him, giving Him all our attention. Can you get on your knees, look up to heaven, and pray to God over the suffering you are going through?

When we follow the examples of when Jesus and His disciples prayed, where they prayed, and how they prayed, God may surprise you in that moment, just as He has done in my life many times. Our goal is to strengthen our relationship with God, and we are learning from God how He can help us during our trial.

What Should Our Prayer Look Like?

Now let us begin to change our focus to our prayer and what our prayer looks like. Before you begin to pray, do you ever sit in silence for a minute or two before you start sharing your prayers with God? I know I am guilty of jumping right in and praying for my own needs and wants. If you wait a few minutes, you may actually hear what God wants you to pray for. In Matthew 6:8, it states that God already knows what we need. We need to remove our own thoughts and desires to hear God through the Holy Spirit.

When we give up our prayer to God, we will be more open to hear Him and how we can heal. During the last few years, I have experienced ups and downs from my condition. Many times I have run to God, telling Him, "If only You will do this, then I will be healed." But then God stops me in my tracks. He says, "Wait. Do you trust Me? I already know what you need." God helps me to surrender to Him, and then, the Holy Spirit helps change my thoughts and words in a way that will be pleasing to God.

As we pray, let us not ask for what we want but truly surrender our will to God and see what He does. Let us now look in the Bible for examples of prayers and instructions for how we should pray.

One of the great prayers in the Bible is the Lord's Prayer. Let us read it together:

> Our Father in heaven,
> hallowed be your name,
> your kingdom come,
> your will be done
> on earth as it is in heaven.
> Give us today our daily bread.
> And forgive us our debts,
> as we also have forgiven our debtors.
> And lead us not into temptation,
> but deliver us from the evil one. (Matt. 6:9–13)

What can we learn from the Lord's Prayer? As I read over these verses, the points that stand out to me from the Lord's prayer include:

- God is our Father, and He watches over us.
- We should honor God for who He is.
- We should seek God's will over our own will.
- God provides us with what we need.
- God forgives our sins, and we are to forgive others' sins.
- Stay focused on God and resist any evil desires.

Jesus used this prayer to teach His disciples how to pray. In the first few words of the Lord's Prayer, it begins by acknowledging God for who He is. In the beginning of this chapter, we learned how God is the Father of compassion and the God of all comfort. These qualities of God are so important. During our low points, we desperately need comfort and compassion. We look up to God for answers. We look up to Him as our Father, who is capable of more than we can ever understand.

As we come to God, you may use this as an example of how your prayer can begin by using what we already know about Him:

"Our Father of compassion and the God of all comfort, You know my pain and my suffering, but through my faith I know You are the God of wisdom, hope, power, and strength who fulfills everything in every way."

Many times the words in the Bible have helped me to pray a deeper prayer or have allowed me to create a more meaningful prayer to God. The scriptures in the Bible can be used as a guide to help strengthen our prayers.

Now, do we need to acknowledge Him like this every time we pray?

No, I do not think it is necessary to start this way every time we pray. At times our prayers may need to be quick, and at other times we may have more time to spend with God. But if we are building a strong relationship with God, then I do think we need to be thinking about how we can honor Him with our words and remember to acknowledge Him for the amazing God He is.

Once you acknowledge Him, we can learn from the Lord's Prayer to include these three different parts:

- Thankfulness/celebration
- Confession of sins
- Prayers offered in faith

Thankfulness/Celebration:

As you are suffering from whatever trial you have been faced with, try and push aside feelings of depression, discouragement, anger, or fear. And be *thankful*! This may be a completely new way to approach your situation, but God asks us to rejoice with Him during any circumstance.

In the Lord's Prayer, it says "hallowed be your name." *Hallowed* means honor. We come to God and honor Him. We celebrate Him. We rejoice with Him.

Paul writes, "Rejoice in the Lord always. I will say it again: Rejoice! Let your gentleness be evident to all. The Lord is near. Do not be anxious about anything, but in every situation, by prayer and petition, with thanksgiving, present your requests to God. And the peace of God, which transcends all understanding, will guard your hearts and your minds in Christ Jesus" (Phil. 4:4–7).

We can present our prayers to God with thanksgiving, and when we do, God's peace will come into our hearts and minds. With rejoicing, we will not feel empty, but we will feel the fullness of God, and a calm will overcome us.

If we think of the life of Peter, we know he experienced plenty of suffering, especially for his faith. One of the things Peter teaches us through his suffering is that we can be strengthened in these difficult times and rejoice: "Dear friends, do not be surprised at the fiery ordeal that has come on you to test you, as though something strange were happening to you. But rejoice inasmuch as you participate in the sufferings of Christ, so that you may be overjoyed when his glory is revealed" (1 Pet. 4:12–13).

When we participate with Christ through these trials, it does not feel natural to want to rejoice. Our natural response is to be fearful and discouraged, and to feel hopeless. But when we take this step of faith and build our foundation in God, we learn that His ways are better than ours. We grow more like Jesus Christ as we participate in these trials.

As we listen to Peter's words and obey God, our new response to handling our trial will look different. It may be hard to follow. At first this was not natural for me to do, but I made the shift so my prayer could be more in line with what God wanted me to do. When I began to rejoice in the suffering I was going through, God showed up. I could feel His joy and I could start to see the glory that Peter spoke about in 1 Peter 4. I was at peace with the trial I was facing and content with my circumstances.

As soon as we shift our way of thinking in a positive way, God will begin to heal us. After sharing with God what you are thankful for during your trial, let us next learn about how we can confess our sins.

Confession of Sins

In the Lord's Prayer, there are two parts of confession. The first is to ask God for forgiveness of our own sins, and the second is to forgive others who have hurt us.

When we ask for forgiveness, we begin taking another step toward healing. Healing comes from the whole body. If we have been hurt by our own sins or hurt by others, we begin carrying around that pain. Those emotional wounds begin affecting our physical bodies.

In Acts 3:19 Peter addresses the men of Israel, saying "Repent, then, and turn to God, so that your sins may be wiped out, that times of refreshing may come from the Lord."

During the few years after my diagnosis, the circumstances that I was walking through made me feel far from God. I was struggling to trust God through my trials. As I prayed, I felt prompted by God to take another step in my faith: "Repent and be baptized, every one of you, in the name of Jesus Christ for the forgiveness of your sins. And you will receive the gift of the Holy Spirit" (Acts 2:38).

If I am going to be created to be the person God wants me to be, then I need to follow and obey the words of God. I chose to obey and take this next step of asking God for forgiveness. On Easter a few years back, I was baptized and began putting my full trust in God rather than navigating through life on my own. I began learning how to let go of the things I could not control. When I was baptized and let go of the unknowns of our infertility and adoption journey, I felt refreshed. I felt like I could have a new start with God.

Like I mentioned before, this journey will be tough. God does not expect us to be perfect and realizes we can get sidetracked at times. But growing in our faith means working hard to stay on track and focused on Him. We must stay even more focused on God and present during our trials.

The Lord asks us to let go of our sins and to be free from them. God is very clear here when He tells us that when we obey His commands and walk by faith with Him, our sins will be wiped clean: "Come now, let us settle the matter," says the LORD. "Though your sins are like scarlet, they shall be as white as snow; though they are red as crimson, they shall be like wool" (Isa. 1:18).

In 2 Chronicles 7:14–16, the Lord appears to Solomon after he finished the temple of the Lord. The Lord tells him,

> If my people, who are called by my name, will humble themselves and pray and seek my face and turn from their wicked ways, then will I hear from heaven, and I will forgive their sin and will heal their land. Now my eyes will be open and my ears attentive to the prayers offered in this place. I have chosen and consecrated this temple so that my Name may be there forever. My eyes and my heart will always be there.

God deeply longs for a close relationship with us and asks for our faithful obedience. God asks us to humble ourselves. He asks us to confess our sins. When we confess our sins, we are following God's commands, and this pleases Him. Remember, God does not keep a tally of our sins, and this verse in Hebrews helps us to understand this: "Then he adds: 'Their sins and lawless acts I will remember no more'" (Heb. 10:17).

Once you are honest with God, then His eyes and ears will be open to see and hear your prayer. This is an essential part of our healing and relationship with God. This step of confession allows us to grow and learn from God that through His forgiveness, we can also forgive each other.

You may find forgiving another person a harder obstacle. In the parable of the unmerciful servant in Matthew 18, verses 21–35, Jesus helps us to understand the importance of forgiveness and how to have mercy on one another. Peter asks Jesus how many times he should forgive his brother when he sins against him. Jesus answers, "seventy-seven times." *Seventy-seven* times? Not once or twice but seventy-seven times. This is an important concept to understand. If God is continuously forgiving us, we need to be able to forgive others continuously.

In this parable Jesus tells us how the king wanted to settle an account with his servant. The servant owed him ten thousand talents, but the servant was unable to pay. The servant fell on his knees and asked the king to have mercy on him. The master took pity on him and canceled his debt.

Through these verses we learn the process of forgiveness:

1. Identify whom you need to forgive.
2. Determine what they took from you or what they owe you.
3. Cancel the debt.
4. Let go and move on.

The last step may be the most difficult. When there is pain associated with a memory, it is harder to let it go. If you are struggling with this part, I would suggest asking God to help you. Every time it comes to your mind, pray to God and ask God for healing in this area of your life. Then pray for the person that hurt you or made you angry. Praying for that person will help you to start to release that hurt to God and help prevent bitterness from taking root in your heart.

In college I was holding on to pain from a past relationship. It was very hard to let go and move on, but once I took these steps of forgiveness and prayed for this person, I felt free from this pain. I could let my heart heal. In Ephesians 4:31–32 it states, "Get rid of all bitterness, rage and anger, brawling and slander, along with every form of malice. Be kind and compassionate to one another, forgiving each other, just as in Christ God forgave you."

God's desire for us is to grow more spiritually. Are you ready to be free from your sins? Are you ready to be free from the pain that others may have caused you?

In James 5:15–16, it says: "And the prayer offered in faith will make the sick person well; the Lord will raise them up. If they have sinned, they will be forgiven. Therefore confess your sins to each other and pray for each other so that you may be healed. The prayer of a righteous man is powerful and effective."

We can be healed from this pain when we confess our sins and work through the pain that others have caused us. If this is an area in your life that you are struggling with on your own, I highly recommend speaking to a Pastor or Christian Counselor. God will lead you to the right person when you seek His help. If you are not sure where to turn, I would first seek guidance from the staff at your church. And when you do find someone to help you, remember that forgiveness takes time. The pain may not disappear overnight, but allowing God to help you work through it can help you to heal quicker.

Prayers Offered in Faith

When you took a step of faith, you made a commitment to God. As we go forward, we are showing God that we will live by

His ways and obey His commands. Our prayers offered in faith take on a new meaning. We are submitting to God and asking for His will over our troubles and trials in our life.

In 1 Kings 8 the Lord told David that his son, Solomon, would build a temple for God. This promise was achieved, and King Solomon carried out the plan. After the temple was finished, Solomon came before the people of Israel and prayed a blessing over the temple. This became known as Solomon's Prayer of Dedication. Why is this important? The importance of this prayer allows us to see how Solomon prayed to God. Solomon approaches God by first kneeling with his hands spread out toward heaven. Then he begins by saying, "LORD, the God of Israel, there is no God like you in heaven above or on earth below—you who keep your covenant of love with your servants who continue wholeheartedly in your way. You have kept your promise to your servant David my father; with your mouth you have promised and with your hand you have fulfilled it—as it is today" (1 Kings 8:23–24).

As Solomon begins this prayer, we see how he honors God and celebrates God for fulfilling His promise. As he continues to pray over the temple, he asks God to hear the prayers of the people of Israel. Solomon acknowledges that when disaster and disease come, then his people should seek God. He asks that God will hear their cries as long as their hearts are right with Him:

> And if they turn back to you with all their heart
> and soul in the land of their enemies who took
> them captive, and pray to you toward the land
> you gave their ancestors, toward the city you
> have chosen and the temple I have built for
> your Name; then from heaven, your dwelling

place, hear their prayer and plea, and uphold
their cause. And forgive your people, who have
sinned against you; forgive all the offenses they
have committed against you, and cause their
captors to show them mercy. (1 Kings 8:48–50)

At the end of the prayer, Solomon asks God to turn their hearts toward Him and help them to obey His words. These verses can help us too. If you are praying over your trial and seeking God's will, remember God sees your heart. We must have our heart and mind right to allow God to intercede in our lives.

Romans chapter 8, verses 26–28, says, "In the same way, the Spirit helps us in our weakness. We do not know what we ought to pray for, but the Spirit himself intercedes for us through wordless groans. And he who searches our hearts knows the mind of the Spirit, because the Spirit intercedes for God's people in accordance with the will of God."

God is transforming our hearts and minds to reveal His will for us. We must listen to God. In our transformation we will see a change in our hearts. We will see a change in our minds. We will see the Spirit intercede in our lives.

When my husband and I were struggling with infertility, I was longing to have a baby, but I forgot about these important commands of God:

- To praise and thank God for my blessings
- To confess my sins and ask for forgiveness
- To seek God's will over mine

I was so focused on what I wanted that I was not surrendering my plans to God. I was sad and upset over my inability to bear a child, instead of thanking God for the good I had in my life. I was wanting to step in and "help" God answer my prayer. I was wanting my prayer to be answered in my timing and not God's timing. I share all of this with you because I learned a hard and important lesson. My plan did not work. My plan did not line up with God's plan. I failed to ask God what His purpose was for our family: "You desire but do not have, so you kill. You covet but you cannot get what you want, so you quarrel and fight. You do not have because you do not ask God. When you ask, you do not receive, because you ask with wrong motives, that you may spend what you get on your pleasures" (James 4:2–3).

When you come to God, check in with yourself to see if your heart is in the right place. We have many desires and wants, but it may not necessarily be what we need. God knows what we need. In Proverbs 19:21 it tells us: "Many are the plans in a person's heart, but it is the LORD's purpose that prevails."

I began learning how to come to God. I began learning how to ask God for His will. I began changing the way I approached my trial. And as I did, God showed us part of His plan for our family.

God blessed my husband and I with a beautiful brown-eyed baby girl through adoption. We named her after my mother, Patricia Lynn. Oh, how grateful we are for our sweet, loving, and outgoing little girl, and as we look back, we can see how God chose her to be a part of our lives.

It may be hard to see while you are in the midst of your trial, but God does have a plan for you. Do you believe God has a purpose through your suffering? What can you learn from the verse in Proverbs 19? What can you learn from the Lord's Prayer? How can all of this help you during your trial?

What we learn is that God's purpose and plan will prevail. We need to trust Him, and when we do, we may be able to see His plan more clearly. When we remain in God and God's words remain in us, our plans will line up together. We will know what to ask God for and He may bless us: "If you remain in me and my words remain in you, ask whatever you wish, and it will be done for you" (John 15:7).

The story of Hezekiah in the Bible is a great example of finding God's will and purpose through prayer as God healed him. This story is mentioned in 2 Kings 18–20 and Isaiah 37–38. Due to the length of the story, I will share only parts of it here, but when you have more time, I highly recommend reading all of it.

Hezekiah became king when he was twenty-five years old and reigned in Jerusalem for twenty-nine years. He trusted in the Lord and obeyed God's commands. The prophet Isaiah was a messenger between Hezekiah and God. One day after Hezekiah had become ill, Isaiah told him, "Put your house in order, because you are going to die; you will not recover" (Isa. 38:1).

Wow, those are some tough words to hear. But after hearing this, do you think Hezekiah ignored Isaiah's words and went on his own way? No, he did not. He immediately prayed to God, "Remember, LORD, how I have walked before you faithfully and with wholehearted devotion and have done what is good in your eyes" (Isa. 38:3).

The Lord responded to Hezekiah's prayer by giving a message to Isaiah: "Go and tell Hezekiah, 'This is what the LORD, the God of your father David, says: I have heard your prayer and seen your tears; I will add fifteen years to your life. And I will deliver you and this city from the hand of the king of Assyria. I will defend this city'" (Isa. 38:5–6).

Isaiah prepared a poultice of figs and applied it to Hezekiah's boil, and he recovered.

In this amazing story of faithfulness and healing, we see the power and goodness of God, but then we also see how God transformed Hezekiah's heart to share God's glorious ways.

Here is a letter from Hezekiah that was written after he recovered from his illness. Look carefully at Hezekiah's perspective of his suffering:

I said, "In the prime of my life
must I go through the gates of death
and be robbed of the rest of my years?"
I said, "I will not again see the Lord himself
in the land of the living;
no longer will I look on my fellow man,
or be with those who now dwell in this world.
Like a shepherd's tent my house
has been pulled down and taken from me.
Like a weaver I have rolled up my life,
and he has cut me off from the loom;
day and night you made an end of me.
I waited patiently till dawn,
but like a lion he broke all my bones;
day and night you made an end of me.
I cried like a swift or thrush,
I moaned like a mourning dove.
My eyes grew weak as I looked to the heavens.
I am being threatened; Lord, come to my aid!"
But what can I say?
He has spoken to me, and he himself has done this.
I will walk humbly all my years
because of this anguish of my soul.

Lord, by such things people live;
and my spirit finds life in them too.
You restored me to health
and let me live.
Surely it was for my benefit
that I suffered such anguish.
In your love you kept me
from the pit of destruction;
you have put all my sins
behind your back.
For the grave cannot praise you,
death cannot sing your praise;
those who go down to the pit
cannot hope for your faithfulness.
The living, the living— they praise you,
as I am doing today;
parents tell their children
about your faithfulness.

The Lord will save me,
and we will sing with stringed instruments
all the days of our lives
in the temple of the Lord. (Isa. 38:10–20)

From this passage we can see the three parts of prayer that we discussed previously: praising God, forgiveness of sins, and a faithful heart that waits patiently for God's will. In this story God restored Hezekiah and added fifteen years to his life, and God's glory reigned and His faithfulness was shared among all the nations.

As our foundation grows stronger, we feel a greater connection with God. We are lifted up a little closer to God's light.

We see our blessings overflowing. We see forgiveness of our sins and we offer forgiveness to others. We begin to see God's purpose being revealed to us. *And through our prayer time, we learn how to be patient.* We take another step and look up to heaven with open arms...waiting patiently for God's answer and purpose during our trial:

"Wait for the LORD;
be strong and take heart
and wait for the LORD" (Ps. 27:14).

A Prayer to Say to God:

God of comfort and compassion,
I come to You and bow down before You. I thank You for providing comfort for me and for never leaving my side. During my struggles, I look to You and seek Your face. I ask for You to help me learn how to forgive, and I ask for Your forgiveness over my words and actions that have not been pleasing to You. Help me, as I take another step, to seek Your will over my trial and show me how I can heal. Lord, I wait for You; I wait for You. Amen.

Week 2: The Power of Seven Challenge

- **Read it, ponder it, and apply it**
- **For the next seven days, focus on your prayer time with God. On each day of the week, open your Bible to *read* the verse listed. Then *ponder* it and answer the daily question. At the end of the week, *apply* what you have learned and come up with a plan to help yourself grow closer to God.**

Day 1

- Read: Psalm 61:1–3
- Daily Question: What other qualities or words can you find in the Bible to describe God that are important in your healing?

Day 2

- Read: Acts 16:25–34
- Daily Question: Is there a time that is best to pray? When is the best time for prayer for you?

Day 3

- Read: Luke 22:39–44
- Daily Question: Do you have a place you like to pray?

Day 4

- Read: Psalm 95:1–7
- Daily Question: Do you have a specific way to pray? Do you ever kneel when you pray?

Day 5

- Read: Psalm 86:6–13
- Daily Question: How can you rejoice in your sufferings?

Day 6

- Read: Luke 18:9–14
- Daily Question: What sins do you need to ask God to forgive? Who do you need to forgive?

Day 7

- Read: Psalm 41:1–4
- Daily Question: What big prayer are you asking God to answer during your journey? Have you been seeking God's will?

Apply It: How Can You Grow Closer to God's Light?

1. What small step can you take this week to have a deeper connection with God through your prayer time?
(Ex. Wake up ten minutes early and spend time in prayer)

2. What big step can you take over this year to have a deeper connection with God through your prayer time?
(Ex. Find a place to pray and kneel)

3. How can you carry out your plans?
(Ex. Add this time to the calendar; designate a room or area in the house)

3

MEDITATION

"I meditate on your precepts and consider
your ways."

Psalm 119:15

D o you feel your roots grasping on to God? Have His
words been speaking directly to you? Have you seen
any growth or transformation in your healing?

In the last chapter, we learned how to communicate
through prayer, and now, in this chapter, we will learn how to
meditate on God's word. Our foundation must stand on the
truth of the Bible. We need to be anchored to His words, and
as our roots spread, our knowledge of Him grows. If God calls
us to meditate on His words, what does that mean?

Meditation is different from prayer. How? I believe meditation allows us to focus on particular verses of the Bible and
helps us to clear our mind to listen to what God wants to reveal

55

to us. One might ask, "How do I begin to hear the words of our Father? How do I know He is speaking to me? How does meditation promote healing?"

These are all great questions. One common problem I found when I was trying to listen to God was the busyness of *life*. When I thought about my day, I saw it was filled to the max by all kinds of activities, chores, and work. I barely had any time to sit down.

What does your schedule look like? Do you feel you are constantly running from one thing to the next? Do you feel absorbed in the busyness of the world? Our lives are filled with one activity after another, working long hours, and being tied to technology. When you sit down to have intentional time with God, how often are you faced with disruptions and distractions? The busyness of daily life has overtaken our time with God. If God is going to speak to us and we are going to hear Him, we must slow down and meditate on His word. If we are going to overcome our trial, we must clear a path to hear God's plan for healing for us.

When we meditate on God's word, we help to clear our mind from our own thinking to God's perspective. We can become very easily affected by the words and actions of others, the thoughts from our own mind, and the circumstances we are going through, such as the trial we are facing. But Jesus tells us, "I am the way and the truth and the life. No one comes to the Father except through me" (John 14:6).

Jesus is our way to God, and the Holy Spirit guides us along the way. When we stop for a moment, we can find God's truth by devoting ourselves to public reading of scripture (1 Tim. 4:13).

From the time we rise to the time we lay our head on our pillow, God's words must be present throughout the day.

Instead of letting outside factors affect us, we invite God into our day and delight in His ways: "Blessed is the one who does not walk in step with the wicked or stand in the way that sinners take or sit in the company of mockers, but whose delight is in the law of the LORD, and who meditates on his law day and night" (Ps. 1:1–2).

One thing I have noticed about our society today is that we spend way too much time striving for the next best thing: new car, better job, bigger house, etc. But who is striving to make their relationship with God stronger? Have you ever thought about it that way? If we put our extra time into godly things, such as prayer and meditation, then what do you think the outcome might be? Would that outcome not be pretty amazing?

We know we want God to speak to us. We know we want to experience something amazing. So, how do we begin to have quiet time with God?

Very simply, we need God front and center in our lives during our trials. We need to come to God and surrender to Him. One Saturday night in August, God met me where I was. God showed up, and I had an incredible encounter with Jesus that I will never forget. It is through my story that I hope you will find encouragement that you could also come face-to-face with Jesus during your journey. After I share more about my story, I will then break down the benefits of meditating on God's word and how it can be a part of our daily lives.

During 2016 my symptoms of PCOS seemed to be more out of control than normal, and I struggled to get them in order. We had just moved to a new state, and of course looking for a doctor to help manage these symptoms was a difficult task in itself. But when I found someone who was knowledgeable about this condition, I accepted her advice to give acupuncture a try to help with this hormonal imbalance. I was not new to this treatment, as I had tried it when I was first diagnosed with PCOS, but things turned out differently this time. On my third visit for acupuncture, I decided to go in the morning before I went to work. During the middle of my appointment, my heart began racing and I felt very strange. The acupuncturist checked my pulse and it was normal. As I began driving to work after the appointment was over, I started having trouble breathing and felt dizzy. I pulled over several times hoping I would not pass out. I made it to work that day, but these symptoms continued, and I went to the ER twice in that first week after the acupuncture. The ER referred me to a cardiologist, neurologist, and ENT specialist. No doctor could explain why I was experiencing heart palpitations, dizziness, and a feeling of overstimulation from sounds and my environment. All my labs and tests came back normal.

The next few months were exceedingly difficult. I was scared. I was letting fear take over my thoughts. Every worrisome thought crossed my mind. When you are faced with a situation like this or if you have been recently diagnosed with a disease, it is hard not to let fear creep in. You think, *What if this? What if that?* But I knew I had to return to the foundation I had built to help me through this tough time. A foundation of faith, prayer, and meditating on God's truth. I had to rely on God.

After four months my symptoms had slowly started to diminish with proper care, and I thought I was in the clear until one night at church. My husband, daughter, and I decided to attend church on Saturday evening. Phil Wickham was opening for our service, and we decided to pick seats in the fourth row. As he began playing, the loudness of the music began to overwhelm my system. I became very disoriented and fatigued. We headed to the back of the sanctuary to find seats, and I barely made it through the sermon that evening. I could not think clearly, but one important point from my pastor's sermon stayed with me through the night: to be thankful during your trials.

Upon arriving home, I told my husband that I needed to rest and asked if he could take our daughter to bed. I headed up to our bedroom, closed the door, and kneeled down. I tried to close my eyes, but they would not stop flickering. I began praying out loud to God and praising Him despite what I was going through (remembering what I learned from the sermon that night). Then suddenly a shadow fell upon me.

I felt Jesus's presence.

I smiled in awe and then became flooded with emotion.

I asked if it was Jesus and felt the confirmation that it was Him.

I told Him how much I loved Him.

Joy consumed me.

A *joy* I had never felt before.

Then for another quick moment, I felt my mother's presence and I told her I loved her.

Jesus's presence was still with me, and I felt His hands on my back.

I asked if He healed me, and *I experienced an incredible light.*

Just as the title of this book reads—*Lift Me Up to Your Light, Lord*—we believe God and Jesus are the light we are searching for. Our journeys are tough, and we need God to lift us up. We look up to God and see His light. His incredible light is what we seek. God showed me His light, and in that moment with Jesus, I wanted to hold on to it forever.

The amazing thing is we can all walk in God's light today, tomorrow, and always.

Jesus tells everyone, "I am the light of the world. Whoever follows me will never walk in darkness, but will have the light of life" (John 8:12).

That night when I kneeled down and thought I was among the darkness, God's light lifted me up. I was able to receive a glimpse of what it is like to be next to Jesus and a healing embrace that took away the suffering I was facing at that moment.

If you have not had an encounter with God and Jesus, you may long to have one. You may long to come face-to-face with Him. In my own experience, our time to come to Him is right now. We do not have to wait. And trust me, when you see His light, you may be like me, wanting to come back for more and more.

As a follower you believe He can do what He says He will. You believe in His truth.

We wake up with God in our thoughts, God in our hearts, and God's words in our mouths:

> The path of the righteous is like the morning sun, shining ever brighter till the full light of day. But the way of the wicked is like deep darkness; they do not know what makes them stumble. My son, pay attention to what I say; turn your ear to my words. Do not let them out of your sight, keep them within your heart; for they are life to those who find them and health to one's whole body. (Prov. 4:18–22)

God is instructing us to open up our Bible every day and listen closely to His words. God is the light to our path. God is the light to our healing. God is here to teach us all that we need to know: "Listen, my sons, to a father's instruction; pay attention and gain understanding. I give you sound learning, so do not forsake my teaching" (Prov. 4:1–2).

During our healing journey, we are focusing on our whole being: our mind, body, and soul. We need to know how meditating on God's word is "health to one's whole body" and what benefits it can bring to us: "Praise the LORD, my soul; all my inmost being, praise his holy name. Praise the LORD, my soul, and forget not all his benefits" (Ps. 103:1–2).

Over the years I have learned of the many benefits to meditating on God's word and why it is important to keep Him front and center over our lives. During the rest of this chapter, I will discuss each of these benefits. As you read through them, think about what area you may need help with and remember our paths will be straighter when we follow God's word with these truths in our hearts:

- We can gain knowledge of God.
- We can find refuge in God.
- We can learn to apply wisdom from God.

Knowledge of God

In the last two chapters, we have been learning about a God who performs miracles, accomplishes great things among the people that He has chosen, and openly shares those stories with us: "All Scripture is God-breathed and is useful for teaching, rebuking, correcting and training in righteousness" (2 Tim. 3:16).

God's words have been carefully chosen and set before us in the Bible. Each story in the Bible is significant. These stories have been passed down from generation to generation. We learn through the stories of Moses, Aaron, Jacob, and other key individuals who God is, how He was present in their lives, and what He was able to accomplish through them. As we meditate on these stories, we see how our Holy God is so great:

> I will remember the deeds of the LORD; yes, I will remember your miracles of long ago. I will consider all your works and meditate on all your mighty deeds. Your ways, God, are holy. What god is as great as our God? You are the God who performs miracles; you display your power among the peoples. With your mighty arm you redeemed your people, the descendants of Jacob and Joseph." (Ps. 77:11–15)

God's promise to Moses, Aaron, and Jacob has never changed. We know God never left them, and He restored them into strong and faithful leaders. During our trials we must turn to these stories. Many of them had troubles and difficulties just like us. They have been through it and have come out on the other side. They have taught us to keep God's word as a lamp for our feet and a light for our path (Ps. 119:105).

When our mind is surrounded by the stories of the Bible and the truth of the scriptures, our soul will begin to ask for more: "I remember the days of long ago; I meditate on all your works and consider what your hands have done. I spread out my hands to you; I thirst for you like a parched land" (Ps. 143:5–6).

On days when I have not picked up my Bible or focused on scripture verses throughout the day, my mind is focused only on myself and the activities of the day. It is difficult to block negative thoughts from coming in, and my faith does not feel as strong. But on the days when I do become absorbed in the word of God, those are the days I feel the closest to God. My soul naturally reaches out for more so I can learn more about Him and grow wiser in my judgment.

Refuge in God

When we dwell on the health issue or trial we are facing, we surround ourselves with negative thoughts. Our minds can easily wonder and cause us great anxiety throughout the day and night, just like David's did: "My heart is in anguish within me; the terrors of death have fallen on me. Fear and trembling have beset me; horror has overwhelmed me" (Ps. 55:4–5).

In Psalm 55 David at first wanted to run away from these thoughts and feelings. But we do not have to run. We do not have to hide. We need to come to God. Later in that chapter, David acknowledges these feelings and remembers where his focus needs to be: "As for me, I call to God, and the LORD saves me. Evening, morning and noon I cry out in distress, and he hears my voice" (Ps. 55:16–17).

At times these negative feelings and thoughts may be all we can think about. But if we are going to be able to overcome this, we must keep God's truth in our hearts: "May these words of my mouth and this meditation of my heart be pleasing in your sight, LORD, my Rock and my Redeemer" (Ps. 19:14).

After my encounter with Jesus, I had more energy and I was feeling better, but I was still struggling with negative thoughts. One week later my husband left for an overnight work trip. As I felt alone that evening, I felt fear start to creep in. *What if these symptoms would come back? What if something happened to me when my husband was gone?* I could not fall asleep, and my husband stayed on the phone with me late into the night. The fear caused panic to overcome me. I had never experienced this before. But as I woke up the next morning, I opened my Bible and Psalm 57 spoke to me.

Verses 1-6 say,

> Have mercy on me, my God, have mercy on me,
> for in you I take refuge.
> I will take refuge in the shadow of your wings
> until the disaster has passed.
> I cry out to God Most High,
> to God, who vindicates me.
> He sends from heaven and saves me,
> rebuking those who hotly pursue me—
> God sends forth his love and his faithfulness.
> I am in the midst of lions;
> I am forced to dwell among ravenous beasts—
> men whose teeth are spears and arrows,
> whose tongues are sharp swords.
> Be exalted, O God, above the heavens;
> let your glory be over all the earth.
> They spread a net for my feet—
> I was bowed down in distress.
> They dug a pit in my path—
> but they have fallen into it themselves.

On this morning I fell to my knees praising God for His word. I felt His wings around me, saving me from my fear and comforting me in my distress. I needed to take God's truth and surround myself with it. When we are weak, the enemy will try to place fear in our minds. He will do anything to keep us away from God, and I could feel I was being tested. The question I needed to ask myself was, *Would I let my mind be influenced by the enemy's lies or would I allow my soul to take refuge in God's truth?*

The enemy can seem like a lion—ready to sneak up behind us when we are not looking and hurt us with those lies. Peter knows what this is like and also warns us. Peter tells us to, "Be alert and of sober mind. Your enemy the devil prowls around like a roaring lion looking for someone to devour. Resist him, standing firm in the faith, because you know that the family of believers throughout the world is undergoing the same kind of sufferings" (1 Pet. 5:8–9).

When we believe a lie from the enemy, then our minds become absorbed in that negative thought. However, God wants to speak truth into our lives, and when you keep God's words in the front of your mind, you will be able to resist the enemy's lies and deception. God wants us to be aware of this and alert to those lies.

God is our refuge in our storm. We may be weak or run down from the trial we are facing, but God tells us to take refuge in the shadow of His wings. I knew after my episode with the acupuncture that I was weak, and I did not want fear to keep following me. I wanted to break free from it. I needed to remove these negative thoughts and replace them with God's truth.

One of the ways I was able to overcome these thoughts was dismissing them and replacing them with godly words. Sounds easy, right? Let me explain. After having difficulty with driving after the acupuncture appointment, I struggled with driving on the highway and longer distances. It was hard not to think, *What if I have an episode of dizziness again? I may not be able to pull the car over in time.* When these negative thoughts would enter my mind, I would respond by speaking to God: "God, I know this thought is not from You; please remove this fear from my mind." Then I would meditate on words from a scripture verse. The Bible verse that was the most helpful for me was "Do not fear, for I am with you" (Isa. 41:10). I would continue to repeat this until the negative thought was lifted. At times I may have repeated this at least five times before God's truth was ingrained in my mind.

It is beneficial to have a verse or two close by to help you through your tough moments. I saw my mom practice this exercise as well as she grew more and more weak from cancer. And as she sought refuge in God through scripture, her faith grew stronger and stronger.

When we begin reciting God's truth, it becomes more natural. We fill our minds and bodies up with God's goodness, and when we do, there is less and less room for the lies of the enemy. We can believe in *truth* and hold tightly to the teachings of our Father: "God is our refuge and strength, an ever-present help in trouble. Therefore we will not fear" (Ps. 46:1–2).

Wisdom from God

As I was sitting here writing this, my husband and I were talking through several big decisions and I was feeling anxious as I tried to process through it. But then I opened my Bible and God helped me realize this: our decisions should not be made without God and the help of our Christian family around us. Let us say you have recently found out you have been diagnosed with (fill in the blank), and your doctor tells you, "Here is the treatment they recommend." As we are faced with this big decision and an urgency to decide what we should do, we need to take a step back. We need to explore all our options. This one decision may feel like it is right in our own mind, but we need to dive into God's insight.

When I was first diagnosed with PCOS and infertility, I sought help from several fertility specialists, gynecologists, and naturopathic doctors, and they offered a variety of treatments. The choice was not easy. But I had to decide what the best line of treatment would be for me and my family. As my husband and I discussed our options, we chose not to go any further with fertility drugs due to my increased risk for cancer due to my mom and aunt's experiences. I then began to seek the wisdom of God and His insight in what other ways would be helpful in healing my condition. I referred to the Bible and read Psalm 119:97–102:

> Oh, how I love your law! I meditate on it all day long. Your commands are always with me and make me wiser than my enemies. I have more insight than all my teachers, for I meditate on your statutes. I have more understanding than the elders, for I obey your precepts. I have kept my feet from every evil path so that I might obey your word. I have not departed from your laws, for you yourself have taught me.

After reading this, I recalled a few decisions when I left God out of the equation, and during those times, I felt distant from Him. I was not spending the time meditating on His word. In those instances the outcomes of my decisions turned out poorly. I chose what I thought was best, and this may or may not have lined up with God's plan.

All throughout our life, we will come across big and small decisions. Decisions that may be related to our suffering and trials and other family, work, and life decisions. In this next simple example from my life, I will share with you a time when

I failed to put God first. Let me tell you what happened and what I learned from it.

One day recently I knew I needed to talk to God about the situation I was trying to handle at work. My plan was to read my Bible before bed, but phone calls got in the way and I was too tired. The next morning I knew I needed time with God and thought I would look for a prayer to start my day. God made it loud and clear what I should do. The first thing I opened said (in large letters), "Girl, read your Bible." I chuckled but then thought, *Okay Lord, I hear You.*

Why is it that we push off our time with God and think we will just do it tomorrow? Why is it that we go to everyone else and rely on our own feelings before coming to God? When God is at our center, He will be the first one we go to. I believe we can all hear God better when we are immersed in His word. We want the word of Christ to dwell in us. We want Him to be a part of our decisions. We know God's words will make us wiser.

We can try every healing trick and every treatment mentioned to us, but if we do not meditate on God's word and seek His truth, we will not have the wisdom to discern the best treatment for ourselves. God tells us if we stay focused on His truth, we can be successful in overcoming many obstacles we face.

Look at how God helped Joshua lead his people across the Jordan River to inherit the land sworn to their forefathers. God said, "Keep this Book of the Law always on your lips; meditate on it day and night, so that you may be careful to do everything written in it. Then you will be prosperous and successful. Have I not commanded you? Be strong and courageous. Do not be afraid; do not be discouraged, for the LORD your God will be with you wherever you go" (Josh. 1:8–9).

Joshua had a big decision on his hands. He was responsible for leading all of his people across the Jordan River. God told him to meditate on His words and He would be with him wherever he went. In our trial we need to meditate on God's words to help us overcome the troubles we are facing. As we are faced with a decision related to our trial, we will be more likely to apply the wisdom of God as we process through it.

God will never steer us in the wrong direction. God's plans for us are well-thought-out, and He tries to point us to the right path. When we are open to listen, God freely shares His wisdom with us. In James 3:17 it tells us, "the wisdom that comes from heaven is first of all pure; then peace-loving, considerate, submissive, full of mercy and good fruit, impartial and sincere."

God's wisdom can guide us during our trial. God's wisdom is filled with all of this goodness. God wants us to be well. He is our answer to how we can find healing. We first must ask Him, and then we must take the time to listen through the Holy Spirit to receive His truth:

> But when he, the Spirit of truth, comes, he will guide you into all the truth. He will not speak on his own; he will speak only what he hears, and he will tell you what is yet to come. He will glorify me because it is from me that he will receive what he will make known to you. All that belongs to the Father is mine. That is why I said the Spirit will receive from me what he will make known to you. (John 16:13–15)

The Spirit of Truth can guide us, and when we seek His wisdom, He can help make our paths straight: "Trust in the LORD with all your heart and lean not on your own understanding; in all your ways submit to him, and he will make your paths straight. Do not be wise in your own eyes; fear the LORD and shun evil. This will bring health to your body and nourishment to your bones" (Prov. 3:5–8).

Do you feel your seed anchored down now by its roots? Do you have God at the center of your trial? Are you ready to obey and trust God? If we simply believe but do not keep in communication with God and search for His wisdom in the Bible, then it will be harder for our seed to rise above and break through the ground. If we follow our own ways and let fear be our driving force, we will not find this Spirit of Truth. Jesus says, "If you hold to my teaching, you are really my disciples. Then you will know the truth, and the truth will set you free" (John 8:31–32).

This verse in John 8 is significant. It helps us see the way toward God's light. When we follow His teaching, He keeps us on track. On the night that I encountered Jesus, God taught me to rejoice in my sufferings. This was a truth I needed to apply in my life, and when I learned that truth, I felt free. I could move past the pain and sorrow I was holding on to.

You see, God will talk to us. He will reach out to us. He expects us to listen to His truth and apply it to our lives: "Whoever belongs to God hears what God says" (John 8:47).

When we clear away our distractions in life and take the time to meditate on God's words, we will hear what God has to say to us. We open our Bible and allow ourselves to receive the word, the truth, and the life. We listen to God and proclaim His word to be true. We accept it and apply it to our lives.

Meditating on God's word has helped us learn of His truth and provided us with the wisdom to make sense of His commands. As we walk feeling surrounded by His wings, let the knowledge and the wisdom of Him continue to guide us as we learn of other ways to care for our bodies during our trials: "For wisdom will enter your heart, and knowledge will be pleasant to your soul. Discretion will protect you, and understanding will guard you" (Prov. 2:10–11).

A Prayer to Say to God:

God of Truth,

I lift up my praises to You and thank You for teaching me, correcting me, and guiding me along my journey. Your word allows me to stand up against fear. Your wings help keep me safe and shelter me during times of trouble. Lord, I ask that You may help me to apply Your wisdom and discern what steps I need to take to heal. I trust in You and look up to Your light every day.

Amen.

Week 3: The Power of Seven Challenge

- **Read it, ponder it, and apply it**
- **For the next seven days, focus on meditating on God's word. On each day of the week, open your Bible to *read* the verse listed. Then *ponder* it and answer the daily question. At the end of the week, *apply* what you have learned and come up with a plan to help yourself grow closer to God.**

Day 1

- Read: Matthew 26:36–46
- Daily Question: How is the busyness of life affecting your time with God?

Day 2

- Read: Matthew 17:1–8
- Daily Question: Have you ever experienced an encounter with God? What was it like?

Day 3

- Read: 1 Peter 1:23–25
- Daily Question: What does "God-breathed" mean to you?

Day 4

- Read: Psalm 27:1–6
- Daily Question: Do you feel like the enemy is trying to keep you from the good of God and from moving closer to your healing? How?

Day 5

- Read: Matthew 8:23–27
- Daily Question: Has your trial made you feel afraid or fearful? Explain.

Day 6

- Read: Proverbs 12:15
- Daily Question: In what situations have you relied on your own feelings? In what situations have you gone to God first? What difference have you seen?

Day 7

- Read: Proverbs 4:1–10
- Daily Question: What truth is God trying to teach you?

Apply It: How Can You Grow Closer to God's Light?

1. What small step can you take this week to gain a deeper understanding of God's word?
   (Ex. Find a verse to meditate on)

2. What big step can you take over this year to gain a deeper understanding of God's word?
(Ex. Pick a book of the Bible and begin reading through a chapter each week)

3. How can you carry out your plans?
(Ex. Write down and memorize this verse; find a friend to read a book of the Bible with you)

4

NOURISHMENT

"So whether you eat or drink or whatever you
do, do it all for the glory of God."

1 Corinthians 10:31

Are you good at gardening? Do you remember to take care of your plants and flowers so they have a suitable environment to live? This may seem like a strange question to ask in a book about healing, but in a way, it is applicable to how we take care of God's land and ourselves. For me this is an area I struggle with. I struggle with remembering to water my plants and flowers daily, and when I do remember, I usually overwater them or do not give them enough water. My plants and flowers do not survive very well in these conditions.

In the past I also struggled to take care of myself and make good choices for my body. My body was run down and depleted of essential nutrients. I could feel the strain I was putting on my body by not taking good care of it. I knew if I wanted to overcome the symptoms of PCOS, I needed to make a positive change.

Think about how well you are caring for yourself right now during your trial. Would you say you are making good choices to allow your body to heal?

Remember, our plant needs proper care to survive the tough conditions it may face. We need proper care to survive the tough trial we are going through. We want our young plant to emerge from the ground stronger than ever. Now that we have gained the tools for spiritual healing through faith, prayer, and meditation, we now begin to focus on our physical healing. For the next three chapters, we will be learning what God teaches us about nutrition, rest, and strength to help us become the beautiful creation God intended us to be. We will be gaining His knowledge and applying His wisdom to help us take care of our bodies.

What we eat and what we drink is crucial to our healing journey. We cannot function without proper nutrition. We cannot survive without proper nutrition. Food and water are essential to our bodies. We may have ignored—or simply did not know—that the food and drinks we consume can have a negative impact on our health. I did not understand this until I faced health challenges. When I first started researching the best foods to help heal my symptoms of PCOS, I noticed the foods that I was consuming had very little nutritional value and I was surprised by how scripture was calling my attention to certain food groups. I was ready to make a change in this area, and I wanted to start eating foods that would help fill my body with the best nourishment.

The approach I took was different from the traditional line of treatment that many may be familiar with for PCOS. I chose to take a more simple and natural approach to see if adding more foods with vitamins and minerals would have an impact on my health. The wisdom and knowledge I began gaining from God kept pointing me toward the foods He created and the pure spring water He brought into this land. I was ready to make a change.

Before I share more about what I learned, I first would like to share a little bit about my background when I was growing up so you will be able to see where I started and how far I have come. As a baby I drank only juice. Milk was not my favorite, so instead I enjoyed apple juice in a sippy cup daily. I grew to be a picky eater and did not venture too much outside of my comfort zone. Occasionally I would eat vegetables such as corn and green beans from a can, but my diet mainly consisted of grilled cheese, chicken fingers, and toast for breakfast. In high school and college, my beverage of choice was Coke, and an easy meal to make was Hamburger Helper or just picking up fast food. I also loved doughnuts...chocolate frosted doughnuts.

When my husband and I got married, I knew how to make about three meals: spaghetti, tacos, and chicken patties in the oven. We had this joke that after I finished grocery shopping, we would see how long the two pieces of red velvet cake I purchased would be able to last. Usually I would have half of mine eaten while putting away the groceries, and if my husband did not eat his by that night, his portion of the delicious cake would be mine.

You see, I grew up eating a lot of processed foods. I grew up eating a lot of sweets. I grew up eating limited amounts of healthy food. My mom and dad tried to offer better alternatives, but I did not have the knowledge to discern what was best for me. I also did not know how my choices then would later affect me.

Today we are all faced with a daily battle of having fast, unhealthy foods at our fingertips. Those sweet, sugar-filled candy bars stare at us in the checkout line at the grocery store. The five fast food restaurants that we pass on the way home from work make it more appealing to stop and eat there instead of preparing and cooking a nice, healthy meal at home. In this chapter we need to keep God front and center over this area because it is probably the most difficult to make changes in. My diagnosis of PCOS helped me change the way I looked at food and drinks. I hope you will begin to take a different approach to looking at food too. As we move forward, we will learn what foods and drinks God has instructed us to consume. We can honor and glorify God by listening to Him and being more mindful about our diet choices. The food that God has intended for us to eat will help us heal and keep us strong during our trials.

When I was ready to make changes to my diet, I first started looking at the first chapters in Genesis and I began to learn how God created a land for us that cultivates real, nourishing foods and overflows with fresh spring water.

Starting from creation, God knew exactly what our bodies needed. God had a perfect plan for how He would create the world. As you read through the verses in Genesis, keep in mind that God had a purpose and a reason why the world was created this way.

The very first thing God created was light. It may be no surprise now that this was created first. We know how God encompasses this great light, and God was able to separate the light from the darkness.

Next God made sky! He was able to separate the water from an expanse known as the sky. "God said, 'Let the water under the sky be gathered to one place, and let dry ground appear.' And it was so. God called the dry ground 'land,' and the gathered waters he called 'seas'" (Gen. 1:9–10).

All of this was so good.

"Then God said, 'Let the land produce vegetation: seed-bearing plants and trees on the land that bear fruit with seed in it, according to their various kinds.' And it was so" (Gen. 1:11).

Next God made animals to live in the water: "So God created the great creatures of the sea and every living thing with which the water teems and that moves about in it, according to their kinds, and every winged bird according to its kind" (Gen. 1:21).

And on the land, "God made the wild animals according to their kinds, the livestock according to their kinds, and all the creatures that move along the ground according to their kinds. And God saw that it was good" (Gen. 1:25).

God created this perfect system that would work together to allow food and water for us, but God also knew there needed to be someone to watch over the animals and to take care of the land: "Then God said, 'Let us make mankind in our image, in our likeness, so that they may rule over the fish in the sea and the birds in the sky, over the livestock and all the wild animals, and over all the creatures that move along the ground'" (Gen. 1:26).

God created man in His own image. But how? "The LORD God formed a man from the dust of the ground and breathed into his nostrils the breath of life, and the man became a living being" (Gen. 2:7).

God did not want man to be alone, so He created a companion for him and called her woman. Adam and Eve were the first two people to walk the earth. The amazing thing is that God made each of us unique, just as He did with Adam and Eve! God had this idea how men and women would look, but

God created each of us with a unique design that is different from anyone else:

> For you created my inmost being; you knit me together in my mother's womb. I praise you because I am fearfully and wonderfully made; your works are wonderful, I know that full well. My frame was not hidden from you when I was made in the secret place, when I was woven together in the depths of the earth. Your eyes saw my unformed body; all the days ordained for me were written in your book before one of them came to be. (Ps. 139:13–16)

From these verses we learn that God had a plan for us long before we were born. Our first job on earth was to rule over all the animals and to take care of God's garden. In God's garden and all along His land, He provides the food and water we need to survive. In this intricate design of the world, He placed everything before us, and it is here to meet our needs. Jesus reminds us of this in Matthew 6, verses 31–33: "So do not worry, saying, 'What shall we eat?' or 'What shall we drink?' or 'What shall we wear?' For the pagans run after all these things, and your heavenly Father knows that you need them. But seek first his kingdom and his righteousness, and all these things will be given to you as well."

God believes each of us is special. He cares deeply about us that He gives us everything we need. God gave us this one life, and He asks us to take care of our bodies: "Do you not know that your bodies are temples of the Holy Spirit, who is in you, whom you have received from God? You are not your own; you were bought at a price. Therefore honor God with your bodies" (1 Cor. 6:19–20).

We received our body from God, and we need to honor God with our body. If we think of our body as a temple, we see it as being strong, but at times it can become weak if it is not properly taken care of.

How do we begin to honor God with our bodies? What we eat and how much we eat affects not only ourselves but God. What we drink and how much we drink affects not only ourselves but God. God wants me to be a strong and healthy Christ follower. God wants you to be a strong and healthy Christ follower. Why? So we can do more of His work here on earth. If we are sick, we lose sight of God's kingdom because we are more focused on the circumstances we are going through. Many times we cannot control an illness or the trials that come upon us, but we can control how we care for our body, and one of those ways is through food and water.

As we look back at the first chapter of Genesis, we see water was present from the very beginning. I feel it is no coincidence that it is mentioned from the beginning of time and then throughout the rest of the Bible 722 times.[2] Water is crucial to our bodies. Why? Our bodies are made up of 60 percent water. This is a significant number, and therefore every day we need to be replenishing our bodies with clean, pure and, if possible, uncontaminated water. Water helps to maintain so many processes within our bodies even down to the cellular level. We need to make it a priority to be flushing out toxins, hydrating our cells, and allowing our organs to function properly to heal.

God painted before us a beautiful picture of how water appeared on land when no other sign of vegetation or life was present: "But streams came up from the earth and watered the whole surface of the ground" (Gen. 2:6).

Water was one of the first essential properties needed to support the lives of plants, animals, and humans. When God created the first two humans to live on land, He supplied them with all that they needed. God placed a river in Eden for Adam and Eve. This river allowed them to water the Garden of Eden (Gen. 2:10). In addition, this river was separated into four parts: Pishon, Gihon, Tigris, and Euphrates. God supplied Adam and Eve with water so they would not grow thirsty, and this water would allow their food to grow.

Later in the Bible, God also used water to show us how it can heal. In 2 Kings chapter 5, we learn of a man named Naaman who had leprosy. When he came to Elisha's house to get help, Elisha sent a messenger to tell him to "Go, wash yourself seven times in the Jordan, and your flesh will be restored and you will be cleansed" (2 Kings 5:10).

Naaman at first refused to do so. He had hoped he would be quickly cured, and he was angry that there was not an easier way. He said, "I thought that he [Elisha] would surely come out to me and stand and call on the name of the LORD his God, wave his hand over the spot and cure me of my leprosy. Are not Abana and Pharpar, the rivers of Damascus, better than all the waters of Israel? Couldn't I wash in them and be cleansed?" (2 Kings 5:11–12).

Look at how Naaman responded. He wanted to be healed quickly. He wanted to take the easy route. He felt the other rivers were cleaner and a better option. He was failing to trust God and did not want to obey God's commands. Do we respond to God this way too? Have you done this during your healing journey? Do we step in and tell God, "Maybe this will be a better way"? Do we think God can just wave His hand over us? You see, we all hope there is a simple trick to heal us. But God is testing us. He is testing our trust and our ability to obey His commands. He wants us to grow from our trials. After Naaman clearly saw what he needed to do, he went and cleansed himself in the Jordan. Naaman's flesh was then restored. Naaman's healing came from God, and God was glorified: "Now I know that there is no God in all the world except in Israel" (2 Kings 5:15).

Through this story, we learn that healing takes time, and one of the ways we can begin healing is by following these principles God has set before us. We can take care of our bodies by drinking clean water and being cleansed through God.

We must lean on God through our trial and follow His principles. At times when we think we do not have all that we need, God shows us we live in abundance when He is present in our lives. God has brought us into an amazing world that He has made for us: "For the LORD your God is bringing you into a good land—a land with brooks, streams, and deep springs gushing out into the valleys and hills" (Deut. 8:7).

In the Bible we see where starvation was an obstacle our ancestors had to face, and we too may feel that we do not have the means to choose the best treatment, the best healthcare, or the best food options for ourselves. But do not let that mind-set hold you back. We first start by incorporating these simple principles that God laid before Adam and Eve and all of creation and take small steps to heal our bodies.

Look at how God can help us find the best nourishment for ourselves. In this next story about Elijah, God provided Elijah with what he needed to survive. Elijah was a man who loved the Lord, and when others were starving and thirsty, ravens brought food for him and "he drank from the brook" (1 Kings 17:6).

When Israel did not have much, Elijah followed the commands of God to be able to have enough food and water. The brook had all the water he needed to quench his thirst, and the birds brought him food to keep him satisfied.

When we follow God's commands, just like Elijah we are given this promise: "Everyone who drinks this water will be thirsty again, but whoever drinks the water I give them will never thirst. Indeed, the water I give them will become in them a spring of water welling up to eternal life" (John 4:13–14).

God tells us we have everything we need. We do not need a special potion to heal ourselves. God not only provides us with the water we need to survive, but He provides us with the gift of eternal life: "'Come!' And let the one who hears say, 'Come!' Let the one who is thirsty come; and let the one who wishes take the free gift of the water of life" (Rev. 22:17).

Let us replenish our bodies with water, and as we do, remember God is offering this gift of eternal life to us. Think of God opening our hands and pouring His water into us: "Here, child, you have what you need." As we drink water, we remember how God brought plenty of water up from the ground in Eden and we thank Him for what we have.

God gives us the power to do as we please with His principles. We can choose to ignore them or we can begin to incorporate them into our daily lives. When I drink water, I think of God. I thank Him for replenishing me with what I need. I no longer feel satisfied with drinking unhealthy, sugar-filled drinks. I want to be filled by God, and I know that when I put water in my body, I am choosing what God created for me.

Now, let us switch our attention to food and take a closer look at what the Bible tells us to eat. For me, when I first started to make a shift toward healthier options, I had to change my focus. I had to move my focus from thinking *What can I not have?* to thinking *What nourishing and healing food does God have for me?*

Seven years ago if I were asked if I felt addicted to sweets, processed foods, and/or fast food, my answer would have been yes. I could have easily raised my hand to all those choices, but the one I struggled with the most was sweets. My body was addicted to sugar, and I felt like I was constantly craving a sweet treat before meals, at meals, and after meals. But you will see that with the help of God and changing my mind-set, I was able to overcome this struggle to help myself heal. God helped me discern what I needed for my body.

Today we understand that times have changed. Food that our ancestors had is different from the food we have access to now. How you prepare food today is different from how it was prepared back then. Let us stop and think about how we can return to the simple principles God created for us.

What was it like for Adam and Eve and the other men and women of the Bible? How is it different for us today? Today we know we have limited time. It is also more convenient to go to the store and pick up items or to grab fast food because we do not have the time to make a healthy family meal. So how do we return to the simple principles that God created to help heal us from the many diseases we are facing right now and strengthen us during our trials?

As we dive more into this chapter, we are going to look at what the Bible tells us we should be eating. God created us with wisdom and self-control. We need wisdom to determine what foods will bring healing to our bodies, and we need self-control to resist the addictive foods that are making us sick.

The Bible tells us we were created from the dust of the ground. If we were created from the dust of the ground, does it not make sense that our bodies would need food from the ground to live? God planted the first garden for Adam and Eve in Eden. In the garden there were seed-bearing plants, trees with fruit, and green plants for food. God gave them all the essential food to live and grow.

When I picture the Garden of Eden, I picture a never-ending array of fruits and vegetables. Not only an abundancy of food but fruits and vegetables that resemble all colors of the rainbow. God tells us it was pleasing to the eye. When I look at a picture of a garden, my eyes are drawn to the nutritious fruits and vegetables, and when I eat a delicious array of vitamins, my body feels good. On the other hand, when you see a table full of fried food and junk food, it may look appealing at first, but it does not have the same effect as the first picture. When you eat this food, your body receives no nutritional value. You feel bloated, weighed down, and sluggish after eating it. When we choose to feed our bodies with processed food, junk food, and fried food, we are taking the chance of increasing the risk of disease in our bodies. God made our bodies to thrive on fruits, vegetables, herbs/spices, grains, seeds, legumes, nuts, oils, dairy, and meat. It is time to change our mind-set. Changing the way you look at food is the first step to eating what God tells us to eat.

Take a moment to go into your pantry and pull out a snack or candy package. Turn over the package and look at the ingredients. Do you recognize the names of these ingredients? Does it look like a food God would want us to eat? When I knew I wanted to make healthy choices and to eat real food to help my body heal, I began cutting out several processed foods. I began buying fewer sweets, and I asked my husband to hold me accountable. It took some time, but as I began using the knowledge to discern what my body needed, I was able to change my thoughts and then change my ways.

I am not always thankful for the symptoms of PCOS, but without my diagnosis, I may not have learned all that I know

now. Thankfully God has blessed us with knowledge and He openly shares His wisdom with us. When I did not know what foods could help heal me, I knew I needed to go to God. When I knew my current diet of processed food and fast food would not help me get better, I looked to God for answers. When I asked, He prompted me to look in the Bible. We may not have all the answers to how or why, but He answers this question: *What? What nourishing food will fill me, heal me, and strengthen me?*

In this next section of the chapter, I will list what food God calls to our attention for healing and share a scripture that is related to that food group. In order to be successful at changing our diets, it is important to understand what food to add and why we should add it. Due to the many foods mentioned in the Bible, I am going to break them down for you and start with the first ever created: vegetation.

Vegetation

Vegetation is simply plants bearing seed and trees bearing fruit. When I think of vegetation, the first foods I think of are fruits and vegetables. But do you know we receive many other nutritious foods from plants and trees besides fruits and vegetables? As I began taking a closer look at what makes up vegetation, here is what I found. Vegetation also produces herbs, grains, seeds, legumes, nuts, and oils.

To help us decide what foods we should add to our diet, we need to look at what foods have been created for us. The amazing thing about God is He provides many various types of fruit, vegetables, herbs, grains, legumes, nuts, and oils to choose from, and each food has unique properties and healing actions. Let us look at each one and see what the Bible says about them. In each section, read the scripture and review the list of foods in that particular group. Think about what foods you currently eat from these lists and make note of which ones you would like to try. Please note, these may not be complete lists. I have chosen the most common ones.

Fruit

"Fruit trees of all kinds will grow on both banks of the river. Their leaves will not wither, nor will their fruit fail. Every month they will bear fruit, because the water from the sanctuary flows to them. Their fruit will serve for food and their leaves for healing" (Ezek. 47:12).

Our Choices of Fruit:				
Acai	Cantaloupes	Grapefruits	Nectarines	Pomegranates
Apples	Cherries	Grapes	Oranges	Raspberries
Apricots	Cranberries	Kiwi	Papayas	Rhubarb
Avocados	Dates	Lemons	Peaches	Star Fruits
Bananas	Elderberries	Limes	Pears	Strawberries
Blackberries	Figs	Mangoes	Pineapples	Tangerines
Blueberries	Gooseberries	Melons	Plums	Watermelons

Vegetables

Then God said, "I give you every seed-bearing plant on the face of the whole earth and every tree that has fruit with seed in it. They will be yours for food. And to all the beasts of the earth and all the birds in the sky and all the creatures that move along the ground—everything that has the breath of life in it—I give every green plant for food." And it was so. (Gen. 1:29–30)

Our Choices of Vegetables:			
Artichoke	Carrots	Leafy Greens	Spinach
Asparagus	Cauliflower	Leeks	Squash
Beans	Celery	Onions	Tomatoes
Beets	Cucumbers	Parsnips	Turnips
Broccoli	Eggplant	Peppers	Watercress
Brussels Sprouts	Fennel	Pumpkin	Wild Greens
Cabbage	Garlic	Radishes	Zucchini

Herbs/Spices

"Woe to you, teachers of the law and Pharisees, you hypocrites! You give a tenth of your spices—mint, dill and cumin. But you have neglected the more important matters of the law—justice, mercy and faithfulness. You should have practiced the latter, without neglecting the former" (Matt. 23:23).

Our Choices of Herbs/Spices:			
Basil	Dill	Lavender	Sage
Cardamon	Elder	Licorice	Saw-Palmetto
Cayenne	Evening Primrose	Milk Thistle	Spearmint
Cinnamon	Fennel Seeds	Nutmeg	St. John's Wort
Clove	German Chamomile	Parsley	Stevia
Coriander Seeds	Ginger	Passion Flower	Thyme
Cumin	Ginseng	Peppermint	Turmeric
Dandelion	Green Tea	Rosemary	

Grains

"Take wheat and barley, beans and lentils, millet and spelt; put them in a storage jar and use them to make bread for yourself. You are to eat it during the 390 days you lie on your side" (Ezek. 4:9).

Our Choices of Grains:		
Barley	Rye	Teff
Oats	Sorghum	Wheat
Rice	Spelt	Wild Rice

Do you see what bread was made of in Ezekiel 4:9? Now think of what it is made of (or go take a look)!

Seeds

"The seed will grow well, the vine will yield its fruit, the ground will produce its crops, and the heavens will drop their dew. I will give all these things as an inheritance to the remnant of this people" (Zech. 8:12).

Our Choices of Seeds:		
Buckwheat	Grain Amaranth	Quinoa
Chia Seeds	Hemp Seeds	Sesame Seeds
Flax Seeds	Poppy Seeds	Sunflower Seeds

Legumes

"They also brought wheat and barley, flour and roasted grain, beans and lentils, honey and curds, sheep, and cheese from cows' milk for David and his people to eat. For they said, 'The people have become exhausted and hungry and thirsty in the wilderness'" (2 Sam. 17:28–29).

Our Choices of Legumes:		
Chickpeas	Lentils	Peanuts
Beans (Red, Black, Pinto, Garbanzo, Kidney, Soy)	Peas	

Tree Nuts

"If it must be, then do this: Put some of the best products of the land in your bags and take them down to the man as a gift—a little balm and a little honey, some spices and myrrh, some pistachio nuts and almonds" (Gen. 43:11).

Our Choices of Tree Nuts:			
Almonds	Chestnuts	Pecans	Walnuts
Brazil Nuts	Hazelnuts	Pine Nuts	
Cashews	Macadamia Nuts	Pistachios	

Oils

"As soon as the order went out, the Israelites generously gave the firstfruits of their grain, new wine, olive oil and honey and all that the fields produced. They brought a great amount, a tithe of everything" (2 Chron. 31:5).

Our Choices of Oils:	
Avocado Oil	Grapeseed Oil
Coconut Oil	Olive Oil
Flaxseed Oil	Sesame Oil

In showing these lists, I hope they help you see all the real vegetation that was created for us. We have variety, and we have flavors, colors, and textures that are all pleasing to our senses. As you think about vegetation maybe a little differently now, follow along with me as we discuss the story of Daniel.

During the life of Daniel, Nebuchadnezzar reigned as king, and he ordered the chief of his court officials to bring men in to serve in his palace. King Nebuchadnezzar was looking for handsome, strong, and smart men, and one of the men who was chosen was Daniel. The king provided food and wine daily from the royal table, but Daniel knew this food would only defile him. Daniel asked the chief official if he could eat only vegetables and water for ten days. For ten days Daniel and the servants tested this out, and "at the end of the ten days they looked healthier and better nourished than any of the young men who ate the royal food" (Dan. 1:15).

How could Daniel and the servants be better nourished?

Many of the foods we eat daily do not come from the preceding lists. When we do not make healthy choices, we do not get the essential vitamins we need to function. I would love to add here all the vitamins, minerals, and healing properties these foods provide us, but if I did, this chapter would be around fifty pages long. Due to your time and mine, I will give you an example of one of the foods listed.

Broccoli is a vegetable and comes from the cabbage family. One cup of broccoli contains approximately fifty-five calories and four grams of protein. When you eat this cup of broccoli, your body will be replenished with nutrients including calcium, vitamin C, vitamin A, vitamin K, folate, potassium, phosphorus, magnesium, and fiber. Not only does it have a variety of nutrients, but research shows it may play a role in cancer prevention, it may lower blood pressure and cholesterol levels, it may support your digestive system, it may slow the aging process, it may decrease dental diseases, and it helps maintain healthy bones.[3] Broccoli is just one of the foods off the preceding lists. What if you begin to add more of these? Think about how you will feel. Think about the benefits it will provide for you.

If we would begin to add these foods back into our meals, look at the impact it could have on our bodies. When I research the vitamins and minerals in real, healthy foods, I see a God who is in control of our lives and the lives around us. I am amazed by God's design. God provided Adam and Eve with all the nutrients they needed, and we have these same foods readily available to us today.

Now let me ask you this: Do you suffer from symptoms of fatigue or anxiety or feel constantly run-down? Or maybe you have other symptoms that could be affected by low levels of vitamins in your body, but these labs have never been checked. Think about it. Could your vitamin deficiencies be a contributing factor to your disease or to why you have not felt better? When I learned I had PCOS, my lab work showed that I was a healthy person, but my vitamin D was less than 20 and my iron levels were low. I also did not feel my best. What I began to learn was that all the antibiotics I took as a child, the medications I had been prescribed, and the unhealthy, sugary, greasy, and processed foods I ate had depleted my body of essential nutrients.

I share what I have learned to show the problems many of us are facing and why our bodies are having a hard time fighting off diseases. I do not want another young woman to suffer from PCOS and infertility, I do not want another loving mother or father to suffer from cancer, I do not want a young student to be faced with depression and anxiety. If we could take control of this area of our lives and make better choices, I believe we could rise above many of these illnesses we are facing and feel better.

Let us change the way we look at our food and honor God by eating the foods He intended. Let us nourish our bodies so they do not grow weak. We ask God to fill us up, and when we fill our lives with God, He gives us His blessings. In Exodus 23 verses 25 and 26 state, "Worship the LORD your God, and his blessing will be on your food and water. I will take away sickness from among you, and none will miscarry or be barren in your land. I will give you a full life span."

In the story of Daniel that I mentioned earlier, Daniel followed the simple principle of eating exactly what God created for us. He ate from the vegetation that God intended to be used as food. Daniel honored and worshipped God by eating clean food, and God blessed him and the other men: "To these four young men God gave knowledge and understanding of all kinds of literature and learning. And Daniel could understand visions and dreams of all kinds" (Dan. 1:17).

Wow! How powerful! Look at how the food helped Daniel.

As we move from vegetation to meat, we see there has been some controversy involving what the scriptures say about meat. Let us first see what the Bible tells us and then discuss it.

Meat

In the very first chapters in Genesis, we learn of the plants and animals God created. Then later in Genesis, we learn of Noah having an encounter with God. During this encounter God gives Noah additional directions of what food is good to eat. God tells him, "Everything that lives and moves about will be food for you. Just as I gave you the green plants, I now give you everything. But you must not eat meat that has its lifeblood still in it" (Gen. 9:3–4).

Through Noah's encounter with God, we learn that most animals that live and move are good for food. However, we should not eat the meat that has lifeblood still in it. Chapter 11 in Leviticus also gives us a clear picture of what food is clean and unclean.

Let us break down each section of Leviticus chapter 11, and remember, these are the rules that were given by God to Moses and Aaron.

What animals from *land* are clean and unclean to eat? Verses: 1–8

- Clean: "You may eat any animal that has a divided hoof and that chews the cud" (vs. 3).
    - o Examples include: antelope, buffalo, cattle (beef, veal), deer, elk, goat, moose, ox, sheep
- Unclean: "There are some that only chew the cud or only have a divided hoof, but you must not eat them" (vs. 4).
    - o Examples include: badger, bear, beaver, camel, cat, cheetah, coyote, dog, donkey, pig, rabbit, rat, weasel

What animals from *water* are clean and unclean to eat? Verses: 9–12

- Clean: "Of all the creatures living in the water of the seas and the streams you may eat any that have fins and scales" (vs. 9).
    - o Examples include: cod, flounder, halibut, salmon, sole, trout
- Unclean: "Anything living in the water that does not have fins and scales is to be regarded as unclean by you" (vs. 12).
    - o Examples include: catfish, clam, crab, lobsters, octopus, oysters, shark, squid

What *birds* are clean and unclean to eat? Verses: 13–19

- Clean: No verse is listed in the Bible, but we know of some clean birds to eat
    - o Examples include: chicken, duck, goose, turkey
- Unclean: "These are the birds you are to regard as unclean and not eat because they are unclean" (vs. 13).
    - o Examples include: bat, black kite, cormorant, eagle, gull, hawk, heron, hoopoe, osprey, owls, red kite, stork, vultures

What *insects* are clean and unclean to eat?

Verses: 20–23

- Clean: "There are, however, some flying insects that walk on all fours that you may eat: those that have jointed legs for hopping on the ground" (vs. 21).
    - o Examples include: crickets and grasshoppers
- Unclean: "But all other flying insects that have four legs you are to regard as unclean" (vs. 23).
    - o Examples include: Mostly all insects except crickets and grasshoppers

What *reptiles* and *amphibians* are clean and unclean to eat?

Verses: 29–38

- Clean: No verse is listed in the Bible, but all are said to be unclean
- Unclean: "Of the animals that move along the ground, these are unclean for you: the weasel, the rat, any kind of great lizard, the gecko, the monitor lizard, the wall lizard, the skink and the chameleon" (vs. 29–30).
    - o Examples include: alligator, crocodile, frogs, lizards, newts, salamanders, snakes, toads, turtles[4]

After breaking down chapter 11, the three questions that still linger in my mind are: 1.) Why did God ask us to eat this way? 2.) Should we still follow these guidelines today? 3.) How will following these guidelines help us heal from our diseases?

In this chapter of Leviticus, the Lord speaks directly to Moses and Aaron. In verses 44–45 He states, "I am the LORD your God; consecrate yourselves and be holy, because I am holy. Do not make yourselves unclean by any creature that moves along the ground. I am the LORD, who brought you up out of Egypt to be your God; therefore be holy, because I am holy."

For the first question—Why does God ask us to eat this way?—I think it is simple. God is our Father, the one we look up to. Just as a parent gives his or her children rules and guidelines to follow as they grow up, God is the ultimate creator and is giving us these guidelines because He loves us and wants to protect us. Could the unclean foods cause illnesses in His people? Yes, I believe so, especially when bacteria can spread easily. Does God want us to be holy like Him? Yes, He does. When we trust and obey His guidelines, we grow closer to Him and can fulfill His mission here on earth.

The second question—Should we still follow these guidelines today?—is tough to answer. Some believe when Jesus came, this allowed us to eat of unclean foods, such as pork. This is where the controversy lies. At times we may not fully understand the scriptures or what God is telling us, but we ask God for His guidance to help us discern what is best for our bodies. In Mark chapter 7 Jesus does give some clarity to this question, and He says, "Listen to me, everyone, and understand this. Nothing outside a person can defile them by going into them. Rather, it is what comes out of a person that defiles them" (Mark 7:14–15).

Continue on...

"What comes out of a person is what defiles them. For it is from within, out of a person's heart, that evil thoughts come—sexual immorality, theft, murder, adultery, greed, malice, deceit, lewdness, envy, slander, arrogance and folly. All these evils come from inside and defile a person" (Mark 7:20–23).

In these scriptures Jesus declares all foods clean. Jesus alludes to the fact that the food we eat does not make us unclean, but our words and actions can affect our spiritual cleanliness. If we are going to be more holy, then our focus needs to be on living clean lives, and again, we need to imitate the way Jesus lived. The guidelines laid out before us by God are important, and Jesus did not come to wipe them out. He teaches us other ways to think about them. I believe Jesus tries to teach others that we should not be too wrapped up in the rules but to seek God's wisdom. For me these guidelines are beneficial. I am trying to keep my body clean, and I do not want to cause additional inflammation or disease. We need to seek God's wisdom to understand what He wants us to eat and what He does not want us to eat. Go and ask God. If you feel God is instructing you not to eat a certain food, then your answer should be clear on what God wants you to do.

This now brings us to the last question: How will following these guidelines help us find healing? I do not know about you, but when my body is faced with illness, it is constantly fighting off the bad bugs. It is exhausting. The last thing I want to put in my body is food that can make it worse. Instead I want to keep a balance of nourishing and healing foods. By continuing to follow God's list, I show Him I am honoring Him, obeying Him, and doing my best to avoid any additional harm to my body. When I eat the meat He intended, I receive the protein I need to build muscle and keep my body strong.

Dairy

Have you noticed a change in the dairy section at the supermarket? When I walk by, I see almond milk, coconut milk, and soy milk mixed in with cow's milk (skim, 1%, 2%). Based on what I know from the Bible, men and women were drinking raw, unprocessed milk from cows and goats: "In that day, a person will keep alive a young cow and two goats. And because of the abundance of the milk they give, there will be curds to eat. All who remain in the land will eat curds and honey" (Isa. 7:21–22).

Dairy		
Almond Milk	Coconut Milk	Goat's Milk
Butter	Cow's Milk	Soy Milk
Cheese	Curds	Yogurt

With God's gift of dairy, we have many things that are made from milk, including butter, yogurt, and cheese. I believe dairy is an important part of our diet because God created a land flowing with milk and honey (Exod. 33:3). However, as you choose your products, use caution and research the products you use. Our goal is to find healing, and we are seeking a diet rich in vitamins and minerals. Again, seek God's guidance and wisdom to know what the best products are for you. I am no longer able to eat as much dairy as I used to because of my PCOS symptoms, but I do try and find a balance that works for my body. At the end of this chapter, I will discuss finding a good balance of the foods God made for us and what is right for you.

Other Foods Mentioned in the Bible

The Bible also mentions three other foods (eggs, wine/vinegar, and honey) that can be healing and are known for their key nutrients. We learned from our preceding list that chickens are a great source of clean protein, but they also provide us with eggs to eat. Do you know an egg provides our bodies with vitamin A, vitamin D, vitamin B12, and folate and has six grams of protein?[5] One little egg has a lot of good in it.

The Bible also mentions wine and vinegar. Like me, you might be wondering if wine is okay to drink. When we are considering if a food is okay for us to eat or drink, we need to look at all the facts. The Bible tells us wine is good on several different occasions. Wine gladdens our hearts (Ps. 104:14–15) and makes our lives more joyful (Eccles. 9:7). In a few different stories in the Bible, we see where wine is used for celebrations or special occasions, such as the wedding in Cana of Galilee and the Last Supper. Another way the Bible tells us wine is helpful is for our illnesses: "Stop drinking only water, and use a little wine because of your stomach and your frequent illnesses" (1 Tim. 5:23). Research has shown some benefits of drinking wine for heart health and for our stomach. But keep in mind, wine is not intended to be abused: "Do not get drunk on wine, which leads to debauchery. Instead, be filled with the Spirit" (Eph. 5:18).

On the other hand, the Bible also speaks of vinegar. We know wine turns into vinegar through a fermentation process and is referred to as sour wine in the Bible. You may not be familiar with wine vinegar, but apple cider vinegar is becoming more and more popular. Vinegar in general has a strong smell and taste. When I have used apple cider vinegar in recipes or to drink for a cold, I have always used a small amount (teaspoon) and I have diluted it in water. It can be very acidic and damaging to the teeth: "As vinegar to the teeth and smoke to the eyes, so are sluggards to those who send them" (Prov. 10:26). Although too much can be damaging to our teeth, I feel a small amount can be helpful for our bodies. For me, I have been amazed by the quick results a teaspoon of apple cider vinegar has provided for me when I have had a sore throat or an upset stomach.

The Bible also mentions honey flowing freely throughout God's land in the scriptures Deuteronomy 8:8 and Exodus 33:3. This is not surprising because honey (in limited amounts) is shown to be good for your whole body: "Eat honey, my son, for it is good; honey from the comb is sweet to your taste" (Prov. 24:13). Honey provides a sweetness our bodies crave. Most of us enjoy sweet foods, and we can find more natural sources of sweetness besides always grabbing for a candy bar or a piece of cake. As I have learned about what foods God brings to my attention in the Bible, I have realized I no longer need the chocolate frosted doughnut I used to indulge in. The candy bars in the checkout line no longer tempt me, and the fast food I smell along my drive home is no longer appealing to me. I am choosing foods and drinks that will help my body heal, and I feel so much better today as I give my body the nutrients it really needs.

When I look at the life of my grandma and the health she is in today, I notice how she has been able to stay strong mentally and physically. She continues to make meals that incorporate the good foods listed previously. It has always been a joy cooking alongside her in the kitchen and learning about these good foods. The two meals I have seen her frequently make during the winter are chicken noodle soup and beef vegetable soup. These soups are made with clean proteins, are filled with vegetables, and contain broths that warm your soul during the cold months. If you are looking for more ways to get the nutrients your body needs to heal, I highly recommend finding some soup or stew recipes that you can make from scratch. If you take the time and plan out your meals during the week, you could easily squeeze in a day with a soup or stew recipe.

Try this: Take your broth, toss a bunch of nutritious vegetables into a pot, add some clean protein, and let it simmer throughout the day. And let me tell you, the outcome will be a delicious meal that can be eaten over several days.

As we ponder all this knowledge about nourishing foods and drinks, we should lastly take a minute to discuss how God calls us to find a good balance. Eating too little can hurt us. Eating too much can be harmful. But if we focus on keeping a balance, our bodies will start to heal. We already know that too much of an unhealthy food can be problematic for our bodies, but also remember a healthier food in large amounts may not be a good thing either. The Bible tells us that "it is not good to eat too much honey" (Prov. 25:27) and "do not join those who drink too much wine or gorge themselves on meat, for drunkards and gluttons become poor, and drowsiness clothes them in rags" (Prov. 23:20–21). Find a balance that will be right for you.

We need to listen to God to know what is best for our bodies right now. I am choosing to trust in His ways and follow His principles because He is the maker of this world. Along my journey of healing, I have come to God for His guidance and I have been seeking His truth. A food that may be right for my body may not be right for another person. In my relationship with God, I listen to Him as He instructs me to eat the foods that are best for my health. We should be careful to not place judgment upon others for what they eat and what they do not eat. Our focus should be more on pleasing God and showing Him our thanks for the food He has created for us. *As I have learned about these nourishing foods and the cool water I drink, I see God provides an abundance for me, and He teaches me to be content with all I have.*

God knows our bodies best, besides ourselves. Is God asking you to make a change? Take a minute to think about what your body needs. It is important for us to know what God is calling us to do to make healthier choices. God wants us to be well, and if you feel as if God is instructing you to make changes in this area, then I would ask for more of His guidance. We will use this knowledge from the Bible to make wise decisions in caring for our bodies. Keep these scriptures close by and use this next verse to help keep things in perspective for you as you allow yourself to get enough rest, which we will discuss in the next chapter. Proverbs 18:15 says, "The heart of the discerning acquires knowledge, for the ears of the wise seek it out."

A Prayer to Say to God:

God of Creation,

Your creation amazes me! Thank You for allowing plants to grow, animals to walk the land around us, and water to rain down on the earth. I appreciate Your gift of food and water. I am fearfully and wonderfully made. Please help me to honor You with my body and treat it like a temple. Help me to incorporate more of Your foods into my daily life and show me what foods will be nourishing to my body to help it heal.

Amen.

Week 4: The Power of Seven Challenge

- **Read it, ponder it, and apply it**
- **For the next seven days, focus on incorporating more of God's food and water. On each day of the week, open your Bible to *read* the verse listed. Then *ponder* it and answer the daily question. At the end of the week,**

apply what you have learned and come up with a plan to help yourself grow closer to God.

Day 1

- Read: Revelation 22:1–2
- Daily Question: Recall what foods and drinks you liked growing up. Now, how much of your food and drinks come from God's land compared to processed food off the store shelves?

Day 2

- Read: Genesis 26:19
- Daily Question: Do you replenish your body with water throughout the day? What other Bible verses can you find about water?

Day 3

- Read: Numbers 13:17–27
- Daily Question: Are some of your symptoms or health conditions caused by your food and drink choices? Do you think adding the right nutrients will help you heal?

Day 4

- Read: Genesis 26:12
- Daily Question: Imagine what the Garden of Eden looked like. What do you picture in your mind? Do you have a garden at home or would you like to start one?

Day 5

- Read: Daniel 10:1–12
- Daily Question: What does the story of Daniel reveal to us? What encouragement does this give us?

Day 6

- Read: Leviticus 11:1–47
- Daily Question: After seeing the list of clean and unclean meat to eat, what surprised you in Leviticus chapter 11? What do you think about these guidelines?

Day 7

- Read: Luke 9:16–17
- Daily Question: What have you learned from the Bible verses in this chapter? How can you honor God and give thanks to Him for your food and water?

Apply It: How Can You Grow Closer to God's Light?

1. What small step can you take this week to incorporate more nourishing food and water into your daily life?
   (Ex. Drink at least six cups of water a day)

2. What big step can you take this year to incorporate more nourishing food and water into your daily life?
   (Ex. Start a garden)

3. How can you carry out your plans?
(Ex. Keep track of how much water you drink daily; Use the foods from your garden and incorporate them into your meals)

5

REST

"Come to me, all you who are weary and bur-
dened, and I will give you rest."

Matthew 11:28

How have you been feeling since giving yourself better nutrients and hydrating your body with water? Can you feel yourself reaching up to God for more of His goodness? If you have started to make changes to your diet, then you are moving in the right direction. Your stem is growing taller, and it is ready to make another change. In this chapter we are taking another step to help our plant produce a leaf. Our bodies now need rest. You may struggle with this next step if you do not know how to give your body the gift of rest. The trial you have been facing may be causing you exhaustion, weariness, and sleepless nights. Through this chapter we will learn what God teaches us about rest and how He gives us a sense of peace when we lie in His pasture.

Our bodies perform many processes, and one that is vital to good health is rest. In God's plan for us, He knew the importance of this, and that is why He designed us to need a period of rest. When a baby is first born, he or she will begin to sleep for around sixteen hours a day. Their bodies need rest for their brains and bodies to grow and develop. Studies have shown how sleep directly affects children's learning abilities and adults' cognitive function. For adults most doctors recommend an average of seven to eight hours of sleep at night. If your body is in constant motion or always thinking, it never experiences true rest. Our bodies cannot heal without rest.

From the very beginning, God taught us through His example: "By the seventh day God had finished the work he had been doing; so on the seventh day he rested from all his work. Then God blessed the seventh day and made it holy, because on it he rested from all the work of creating that he had done" (Gen. 2:2–3).

As we break apart these verses, we understand God worked hard in six days to create the heavens and the earth. We saw in the last chapter how God made the sky, the sea, vegetation, living creatures, and man and woman in six days. If you think about it, we also are working hard throughout the week. Some work forty hours per week, or five days a week. Others may work a different schedule, perhaps a night shift, a twelve-hour shift, or days during the weekend. As a mother or father, your work continues through the evenings and weekends providing care for your family. We may think we have no time to rest, but God set this principle to follow because He knew a time of rest was crucial to living a healthy, successful, godly life.

This principle of rest has always been a hard one for me to follow. In high school I worked hard to get good grades and would stay up late to study. In college I took on extra classes to graduate in three and a half years. During one of those semesters, I had eighteen credit hours on my plate and worked part-time. My bad habits continued throughout my adult life. I stretched myself thin with running too many errands during the day, working forty-plus hours, and completing another degree in two years. Then when my daughter was born, my sleep pattern was disrupted by late-night feedings and diaper changes.

When my body became overstimulated from the acupuncture, it showed me I could no longer go on without quality rest and a good night's sleep. I looked to God to learn more about His principle of rest. God gave me hope that I could regain a healthy sleep pattern and learn to rest peacefully: "Take my yoke upon you and learn from me, for I am gentle and humble in heart, and you will find rest for your souls. For my yoke is easy and my burden is light" (Matt. 11:29–30).

If God is an all-powerful God, why would He show us that He rested on the seventh day? Was He trying to model a pattern for us to follow? If you refer back to the scripture from Genesis 2, we see where God stopped His work for one day. On this one day, He blessed it and made it holy. If we follow His pattern, we should also *stop* and *rest*. In showing us this principle in the beginning of creation, God is modeling an important concept.

Are we following this principle? What is our excuse if we are not? Why is it so hard to honor God and ourselves with a day of rest? Why do we not stop and evaluate our day or week to see what we have on the calendar? What is truly necessary? I may think the item on my list is truly necessary, but if it is taking away from God and my time with Him, then it is not as important as I think it is.

When I have made a to-do list for the day, I have about eight things too many on my list. It is not possible for me to get all of it done, and I am only wearing myself down more. In our season of healing, we need to make an effort to follow God's principle of rest. If I am making choices that will hinder my healing, then I am not following the principles that God has set before me.

So we ask ourselves again, how can we honor God by keeping this day holy and find our rest?

If we look to the story of Moses, we can see that Moses faced a difficult time in Egypt. God called on Moses to bring the Israelites out of Egypt. Moses obeyed God and took the Israelites across the desert. When troubles arose during their journey, who do you think was there to bring them to safety and teach them about the principle of rest? Let us read these verses to find out:

> Then his people recalled the days of old, the days of Moses and his people—where is he who brought them through the sea, with the shepherd of his flock? Where is he who set his Holy Spirit among them, who sent his glorious arm of power to be at Moses' right hand, who divided the waters before them, to gain for himself everlasting renown, who led them through the depths? Like a horse in open country, they did not stumble; like cattle that go down to the plain, they were given rest by the Spirit of the LORD. (Isa. 63:11–14)

In this passage of Isaiah, God was there to bring them across the sea. He guided them and took care of all their needs. In an area where there was little food, God provided the Israelites with manna to eat. Every day manna rained down, until the leaders of the community shared these words from God to Moses: "Tomorrow is to be a day of sabbath rest, a holy sabbath to the LORD. So bake what you want to bake and boil what you want to boil. Save whatever is left and keep it until morning" (Exod. 16:23).

In Exodus 16 the first reference to the Sabbath was made to His people. God did not want anyone to go out on the seventh day. His people were called to a day of rest. For those who obeyed and rested, they found that the manna did not disappear, it did not smell, and there were no maggots on it. Moses told them to eat it, because today was the Sabbath and they would not find any new manna on the ground to go gather. Now, if you read along further in this chapter, we see where others still did not trust Moses and the words from the Lord. For those who did not listen, do you think they found manna when they went to gather it on the Sabbath? No. You are right; they did not.

When I read this story, I found it surprising that Moses's people could not see that God provided manna for two days and they were still unwilling to listen to the requests from God. But then it made me realize, maybe that is me at times. These verses make me stop and open my eyes to how I should be more obedient to the requests of God. When God says He will *provide*...He will provide. When God says *rest*...we should rest.

Thankfully God does not turn His back on us. God reiterates this truth when He shares the Ten Commandments with Moses and Aaron. He gives them these laws to follow and to share with all generations to come. As you scroll down the list of the Ten Commandments, stop and read the fourth one: "Remember the Sabbath day by keeping it holy. Six days you shall labor and do all your work, but the seventh day is a sabbath to the LORD your God" (Exod. 20:8–10).

This fourth commandment instructs us to keep the Sabbath day holy. God blessed this day.

Now, are you wondering what this means for us? How can we follow this guideline today? Are we not honoring God if we take care of our errands, shopping, family, or work on this day?

From the first two books of the Bible (Genesis and Exodus), God introduced the Sabbath to His people. It was started in creation, shared with Moses and the Israelites, and then passed along through their generations. They followed the pattern God had showed them. They worshipped God and observed this as a holy day.

In the New Testament, we see where this principle began to change when Jesus came along. The Pharisees were so focused on the law that they failed to see the full picture. Jesus helps us to see what honors God on the Sabbath in the scriptures of Matthew and Luke. Jesus makes a powerful point about the Sabbath in Matthew chapter 12. He stands up to the Pharisees' remarks after they point out that it is unlawful to pick grain and eat it on the Sabbath. Jesus pushes back on the Pharisees' remarks by providing examples to them. The first example speaks of what David did when he was hungry: "He entered the house of God, and he and his companions ate the consecrated bread—which was not lawful for them to do, but only for the priests" (Matt. 12:4).

Another example that Jesus tells is of a sheep falling into a hole on the Sabbath. Would you not save it? He compares this to if a man hurt his hand and needed Jesus's healing. Jesus asked the man to put his hand out, and Jesus restored it. Jesus tells us that we are still to do good on the Sabbath, and we learn through these scriptures that Jesus, "The Son of Man is Lord of the Sabbath" (Luke 6:5).

In Matthew and Luke, Jesus taught us several key points, including the importance of taking care of ourselves and others on this day. But the most important point to keep in mind is Jesus is, and will always be, the Lord of the Sabbath.

How can we remember that Jesus is the Lord of the Sabbath?

On the Sabbath, Moses and His people gave thanks to God for all that they had. God provided food for Moses and His people in the desert; and God provides us with food, water, shelter, and a means to have all these things. God reminds us to recall what He has done for us, and when we do recall these blessings, we come and rest in His presence. Are you taking time to recall what the Lord has done for you?

Picture yourself stepping outside and taking a deep breath of fresh air. As you stand there, you look up to the sky and then transition your focus to God. You close your eyes and drown out all the sounds and noise around you. The sunlight warms you, and you feel God begin to fill you up with His goodness. As you finish this moment, you feel a sense of peace.

This is a powerful moment. That moment I just described may only take five minutes. Think about what a whole day of resting in God would look like.

We can honor God with our time of rest by allowing Him to oversee our time. We have two areas we need to evaluate: rest during the day and rest during the night. We ask God to help us organize our time better to remove unnecessary distractions and tasks. When we do this, we are making more time for God and His plans. In this chapter we will look at how we can put this into practice to help us experience healing through rest.

We know God values rest, but let us read a chapter in Isaiah to gain more clarity:

> If you keep your feet from breaking the Sabbath and from doing as you please on my holy day, if you call the Sabbath a delight and the LORD's holy day honorable, and if you honor it by not going your own way and not doing as you please or speaking idle words, then you will find your joy in the LORD, and I will cause you to ride in triumph on the heights of the land and to feast on the inheritance of your father Jacob. (Isa. 58:13–14)

By understanding the whole picture that God and Jesus set before us, we should think through how we can apply this to our lives. These verses allow us to evaluate our struggles of time during the week and what our priorities should be. God wants us to put Him first. Are we doing the things that please us or Him? Is it honoring God to have our schedule filled to the max every day? God does not want us to follow this picture-perfect view of doing it all, but He wants us to follow Him. We can honor Him by doing the things that please Him. Our full week of activities that we are choosing to do for ourselves and our kids may not comprise the activities that God needs us to be doing. Let us allow Him to be the keeper of our time.

Before researching God's words on rest, I never thought about taking a day to honor God and allowing Him to help me manage my schedule. We consistently attend church as a family and participate in Bible studies, but when I analyzed my time on Sunday, I saw the gap between my thoughts on time and God's thoughts on time. I had not been reflecting on

God's words from the service and how they could apply to me. I had not reflected on how I could use my pastor's message throughout the week ahead. Maybe if I stopped for a moment, God's plan would be clearly placed before me. Maybe I could experience God's true rest when my priorities were not interfering with God's priorities.

As you look at your life, do your priorities line up with God's plans or with your own plans? When we do not take care of ourselves and stretch ourselves too thin, we lose sleep and we can begin feeling a sense of anxiety. Now is the time to evaluate your schedule. Do you have rest in the equation to allow healing?

We know God is here for us. He shows us these simple steps to allow healing. He provides us with knowledge to help us prioritize our tasks. We know the habits we need to change, and God is patient with us.

Have you ever thought of God as your shepherd? Do you ever feel like His sheep? This concept of God being our shepherd is very fascinating. Do you know Moses became a shepherd? Moses first learned to take care of his sheep, and through those experiences, God taught Moses to be a shepherd to the Israelites.

In the Bible many references refer to God and Jesus as our shepherd, and we are Their sheep: "Know that the LORD is God. It is he who made us, and we are his; we are his people, the sheep of his pasture" (Ps. 100:3).

The funny thing is, as Christians we act like sheep. We gather in flocks and stay close together when troubles arise. When one is sick in our church, we as Christians come together as a spiritual family and provide meals, prayers, and comfort. If the Lord is my shepherd, I do not have to face this illness or trouble alone and I can rest on Him. When I am lost or get off track, God brings me back. Just as a shepherd never leaves his sheep, God never leaves our side.

In the Bible it says, "The Lord is my shepherd, I lack nothing. He makes me lie down in green pastures, he leads me beside quiet waters, he refreshes my soul. He guides me along the right paths for his name's sake. Even though I walk through the darkest valley, I will fear no evil, for you are with me; your rod and your staff, they comfort me" (Ps. 23:1–4).

God is our shepherd. He carries a rod, which protects us, and a staff to guide us. The good news is we can rest in His green pastures, but the problem is we cannot hear the quiet waters because we are so distracted by the noise around us. Jesus has been restoring my soul through the last few years. When I make sure I am fully rested through the night and have time during the week to get refreshed, I am a better person. I am a better wife, mother, daughter, and friend.

How can you be a faithful sheep to God?

Very simply—come to God and follow Him. Then you will find your rest. God's arms are wide-open, waiting for us to stop trying to fight this on our own and to stop wandering in the other direction. When we step into God's presence, we are no longer lost sheep. God calls us, and when we listen, we see more clearly God's purpose and plan for our lives. In these next verses, read them carefully and imagine God as the shepherd who calls you personally by name.

> The one who enters by the gate is the shepherd
> of the sheep. The gatekeeper opens the gate
> for him, and the sheep listen to his voice. He
> calls his own sheep by name and leads them
> out. When he has brought out all his own, he
> goes on ahead of them, and his sheep follow

him because they know his voice. But they will
never follow a stranger; in fact, they will run
away from him because they do not recognize
a stranger's voice. (John 10:2–6)

After reading this story, we see another reference to God/
Jesus as a shepherd. Jesus is our shepherd and we are His
sheep. There are times we hear His voice and come to Him
right away. At other times we pretend like we do not hear
Him. If you read the whole chapter of Exodus 16, you will see
examples of where the Israelites were resistant to Moses and
paid little attention to him. After multiple tests, they learned
to trust Moses and God. We must learn to trust God when He
calls our name and know that He will lead us into a land of rest.

Now that we have reviewed the background of the Sabbath
and understand the importance of finding rest in God, let's
answer this question: If we have plans seven days a week, with
no rest, how will we experience God's healing?

Stop here! Let us read that again:

*If we have plans seven days a week, with no rest, how will
we experience God's healing?*

I see the problem in my life. Do you see it in your own life?
The Bible talks over and over about Jesus healing others. God
wants us to be healed from our sickness. He wants to help us!
God gave us a day of rest!

Why is this so important in our healing journey?

In this next verse from Exodus, look at how the Sabbath is
explained: "Six days do your work, but on the seventh day do
not work, so that your ox and your donkey may rest, and so
that the slave born in your household and the foreigner living
among you may be refreshed" (Exod. 23:12).

The word that stands out to me in this verse is *refreshed*. If we are tired, how are we supposed to be servants for the Lord? If we do not rest, how will we have the strength to carry out God's plans?

For many of us, we are exhausted and stressed, and we do not get enough sleep. Our lives do not need to be overloaded. We have a choice! If you are suffering from an illness right now, it may be beneficial to evaluate your life.

After my experience in 2016, I needed to evaluate everything in my life. I knew I had taken on too much and I felt the burden of it all. It was the stress from schoolwork, overworking, overdoing, infertility, the adoption process, moving to a new state, and a work environment that was not conducive to my healing. When several outside factors bring stress to you, and you are faced with a disease or trial on top of that, it wears you down. We think, or at least I thought, *I can take all of this on. I am a strong woman.* But the fact is that no one can take all of this on alone. God stopped me in my tracks and gave me a wake-up call. I realized this was going to take faith, prayer, meditation, healing food, and now a lot of rest.

I could not be the woman God wanted me to be with those stressors in my life. It began with making it a priority to get enough sleep at night. I had to reevaluate my current life situation. I began making big and small changes to my life.

Here are a few of the changes I made:

- I switched jobs.
- I stopped running errands every day.
- My daughter and I enjoyed simple activities inside or at the neighborhood park.
- I had to say no sometimes.
- I made sure to sit down and have intentional time to rest.

- I turned off all the electronics and got into bed earlier to allow myself eight to nine hours of sleep.
- I took more time to be with God.

Some may say they cannot make these changes, but anything is possible with God. In this season of life, our focus is on healing our bodies. You must take this time now to heal, or it could get worse. If you want to experience healing, getting sleep is essential for your body to feel better.

As I wrap up this chapter on rest, let us ponder these questions:

- What happens when we sleep?
- What role does God play?

In chapter 8 of Ecclesiastes, the writer challenges this idea of what really happens when we are sleeping:

> When I applied my mind to know wisdom and to observe the labor that is done on earth—people getting no sleep day or night—then I saw all that God has done. No one can comprehend what goes on under the sun. Despite all their efforts to search it out, no one can discover its meaning. Even if the wise claim they know, they cannot really comprehend it. (Eccles. 8:16–17)

We have learned in school what happens physically to our bodies when we sleep. Our bodies go through different stages of sleep, which allows our organs to rest and contributes to a healthy immune system. This is key for healing, but what happens spiritually is the question I would like to explore further. In Psalm 121 we learn God never sleeps:

> I lift up my eyes to the mountains—where does my help come from? My help comes from the LORD, the Maker of heaven and earth. He will not let your foot slip—he who watches over you will not slumber; indeed, he who watches over Israel will neither slumber nor sleep. The LORD watches over you—the LORD is your shade at your right hand; the sun will not harm you by day, nor the moon by night. The LORD will keep you from all harm—he will watch over your life; the LORD will watch over your coming and going both now and forevermore. (Ps. 121:1–8)

The idea that God never sleeps is important. Throughout the last few chapters, we have read several Bible verses where God protects us and watches over us, but His protection does not stop when we are asleep. In fact, these next stories give me hope that God may be doing more than I will ever know while I am sleeping at night.

In these next stories that I am about to share, watch for a common theme. These people are believed to be dead, but their spirit returns to them. In two of the three stories, Jesus tells us that the person dead was only sleeping.

Luke 7:11–17: In the town of Nain, Jesus saw a boy being carried out and his mother weeping. Jesus was sad for her because she was a widow and the boy was her only son. When Jesus walked over to the coffin, He told the young man to get up and his spirit returned to him.

Luke 8:49–56: As Jesus was speaking, someone told Him that Jairus's daughter was dead. Jesus responded by saying that if they believed, she would be healed. Once visiting her, Jesus told her family that she was not dead but asleep. Once Jesus touched her hand, her spirit returned to her.

John 11:11–44: In the town of Bethany, Lazarus and his sister, Mary, lived. Mary and her sisters sent word to Jesus that Lazarus was sick. Jesus finished His work and left two days later. When He told His disciples where they were going, He told them their friend Lazarus had fallen asleep, but He really meant he was dead. When Jesus arrived, Lazarus had been in the tomb for four days. Jesus went to the tomb, gave thanks to God, and then asked Lazarus to come out of the tomb. Lazarus walked out at once.

Jesus teaches us a lesson from all three of these stories. When we believe and have faith, we will be able to see the power of God. When our bodies are worn down from a sickness or a trial, our spirit may be lost. But we know that we live through God and He can restore our spirit. After getting sufficient sleep at night and taking time to honor God, let us wake up believing God will restore our spirit and transform us to carry out His work here on earth: "Arise, shine, for your light has come, and the glory of the LORD rises upon you. See, darkness covers the earth and thick darkness is over the peoples, but the LORD rises upon you and his glory appears over you" (Isa. 60:1–2).

What wonderful news this brings us! God's light shines on us and we can feel His glory over us: "Let the light of your face shine on us. Fill my heart with joy when their grain and new wine abound. In peace I will lie down and sleep, for you alone, LORD, make me dwell in safety" (Ps. 4:6–8).

God freely sends His blessings upon our lives, just as He blessed Moses and the Israelites in the desert. *God has blessed us with rest, and through our rest, we find peace.* Our bodies can feel refreshed and restored, and we are ready to find our strength:

> "The Lord is the everlasting God, the Creator of the ends of the earth. He will not grow tired or weary, and his understanding no one can fathom. He gives strength to the weary and increases the power of the weak. Even youths grow tired and weary, and young men stumble and fall; but those who hope in the LORD will renew their strength" (Isa. 40:28–31).

A Prayer to Say to God:

God of Peace,

We come before You and search for Your rest. We thought we were lost, but we know You would never leave us. We thank You for calling each of us by name. You protect us, guide us, and restore our souls. Help us to manage our time better so we may find rest in You.

Amen.

Week 5: The Power of Seven Challenge

- **Read it, ponder it, and apply it**
- **For the next seven days, focus on resting on God. On each day of the week, open your Bible to *read* the verse listed. Then *ponder* it and answer the daily question. At the end of the week, *apply* what you**

have learned and come up with a plan to help your-self grow closer to God.

Day 1

- Read: Exodus 33:12–14
- Daily Question: Are you allowing your body to rest like God intended? How has your trial affected your sleep?

Day 2

- Read: Psalm 3:3–5
- Daily Question: How many hours of sleep do you get at night? Is it restful sleep?

Day 3

- Read: Psalm 63:6–8
- Daily Question: Do you set a day apart for God weekly? If not, what is holding you back from doing so?

Day 4

- Read: Isaiah 60:1–3
- Daily Question: What would a day of resting in God look like for you? Does it look different than before?

Day 5

- Read: Psalm 127:2
- Daily Question: Are your actions during the week helping heal you or causing you more burden and anxiety?

Day 6

- Read: Jeremiah 6:16
- Daily Question: Define refreshed. What would help you feel refreshed?

Day 7

- Read: Ezekiel 34:31
- Daily Question: Have you heard God calling you? Have you listened?

Apply It: How Can You Grow Closer to God's Light?

1. What small step can you take this week to help your body feel refreshed?

(Ex. Take fifteen minutes each day to sit quietly with God)

2. What big step can you take this year to help your body feel refreshed?

(Ex. Schedule big plans in the other six days, and spend a day at home with family)

3. How can you carry out your plans?

(Ex. Find a favorite quiet spot at home; look at the calendar weekly to make time for God and family)

6

STRENGTH

"I can do all this through him who gives me strength."

Philippians 4:13

D o you see a God who is in control?
  With many of my trials being out of my control, I have seen a constant God. I have seen God provide me with the food I need to heal. I have seen God provide me with the rest I need to experience peace. And I have seen God provide me with the strength to carry on in some of my toughest times.

God has given all of us external strength and internal strength. Our muscles allow us to have external strength. What you see on the outside is how much power a person can physically exhibit. Our minds, on the other hand, allow us to have internal strength. Our inner strength comes from within us. We can allow our bodies to push on even when they may not want to.

In the previous two chapters, we have been preparing our bodies for this moment of movement, strength, and power. In chapter four, we saw how food helps many functions and body systems, including our cells, bones, and now our muscles. In the last chapter, we learned how important rest is for our bodies and minds. Do you feel more refreshed and energized now? Are you ready to focus on your internal and external strength?

As you think about your trial, think about what your trial has done to you over time. What has it done to your mind? What has it done to your body? Have you felt weak? Exhausted? Run down? My trial has reminded me of a roller coaster. When I have been at my weakest, I have been at the bottom of the hill. I have struggled to make it up to the top and I have not had the strength to get there.

In Isaiah 40, verses 29 through 31 say that:

> He [God] gives strength to the weary and increases the power of the weak. Even youths grow tired and weary, and young men stumble and fall; but those who hope in the LORD will renew their strength. They will soar on wings like eagles; they will run and not grow weary, they will walk and not be faint.

I do not want to simply *try* to make it up over the hill; I want to *soar* over the hill like an eagle. I will not let my trial weaken my body, soul, and mind, but with God, I will renew my strength.

In our time of healing, our bodies have been learning what it is like to have more rest and better food. We want to change our weakness to have more strength and power. Our bodies should be feeling good. God has been showing us that He has been there for us and is helping us make better choices to take care of our bodies.

Every one of us is facing hardships and difficulties. Life is tough, disease is prevalent, and trials come and go, but we believe God has the strength to get us through these tough times. The Bible shows us He is there for us when we are weak. In Psalm 119:28, it says, "My soul is weary with sorrow; strengthen me according to your word."

We come to God for answers about how we can be strengthened according to His word. It has been through my trial that I realize I am weak. I realize I need a greater power. I need God.

Looking back, I can think about the times in my life when moments did not go as planned—moments of little disappointment to great disappointment. In these moments I felt like my soul was weary with sorrow:

- When I did not pass my driver's test for the first time
- When a relationship ended
- When I did not get a job I had hoped for
- When I received bad test results
- When we had an adoption referral fall through
- When we experienced failed attempts to have a biological child

During these moments I opened my Bible. When I felt like I was at the bottom of the hill, God strengthened me. He spoke to me. His word sustained me and, "That is why, for Christ's sake, I delight in weaknesses, in insults, in hardships, in perse-cutions, in difficulties. For when I am weak, then I am strong" (2 Cor. 12:10).

I believe without those moments I would not be where I am at today. With those hardships and difficulties, God taught me about His strength and how I could have the power to rise above. Think back to the men and women from the Bible who overcame tough times. Would they have been the men and women God needed them to be without those hardships or difficulties?

Many of you know of the story of David and Goliath from church or from Sunday school class. If you have not heard this story before, you can follow along with me here. This story has great significance for us and how it relates to this idea that God makes us strong when we are weak or think we are weak. In 1 Samuel chapter 17 we learn of two important characters of this story. The first is Goliath. He was a nine-foot-tall man who wore a bronze helmet, a coat of scale armor of bronze, bronze greaves on his legs, and a bronze javelin on his back. In addition, he protected himself with a shield. He was ready to fight and wanted someone to step up to fight him in battle. David, on the other hand, was just a young boy. He went back and forth to tend his father's sheep in Bethlehem, but he was curious about this Philistine named Goliath. When David saw others were afraid to fight Goliath, David stepped up and said, "Let no one lose heart on account of this Philistine; your ser-vant will go and fight him" (1 Sam. 17:32).

David tells Saul that he will fight Goliath. Now, by looking at David, he may not have looked like he had the external physical strength to stand up against Goliath, but he knew God would give him an internal strength that would be able to beat the giant. David trusted God and knew God would be there for him, just like He had been in the past: "Your servant has killed both the lion and the bear; this uncircumcised Philistine will be like one of them, because he has defied the armies of the living God. The LORD who rescued me from the paw of the lion and the paw of the bear will rescue me from the hand of this Philistine" (1 Sam. 17:36–37).

When the time came, David began to get ready for battle. Saul dressed David up in armor, but the armor was too big. Instead David took his staff in one hand, five stones in his pocket, and his strong faith in God to battle this giant. David said, "I come against you in the name of the LORD Almighty" (1 Sam. 17:45).

David ran toward Goliath, and with one stone, he hit the giant in the forehead and knocked him down.

In this story we see an impossible task for David to take on. He seems too young and not strong enough to defeat a giant, but God makes the impossible possible. God makes the weak strong. And God promises to strengthen and encourage us, just as He did for David (2 Thess. 3:3). It is through God's spirit that David was able to overcome a nine-foot-tall giant, and it is through God's spirit that we can rise above our trials.

What do you think will happen when we are strengthened through the power of God's spirit?

God did not give David a spirit of timidity, and He does not give that to us either. Instead God promises us a spirit of "power, love and self-discipline" (2 Tim. 1:7).

How great is God? Do you see the great design of God? He did not form our bodies to be made from just bones. Instead our muscles attach to our bones to help us move, and we can strengthen our muscles to grow stronger. I do not believe this trial or illness will make me weak or timid, and I will not let it. I come to God and ask for His spirit of power, love, and self-discipline. Let us see what it means to have a spirit of power and self-discipline and then, later, how we can be strengthened through love.

Spirit of Power

To understand how we can have this spirit of power, we need to go to the source, the maker of all things, God Almighty: "You have made the heavens and the earth by your great power and outstretched arm. Nothing is too hard for you" (Jer. 32:17).

When God is living in us, we can feel His power. We believe nothing is too hard for Him. We trust Him, even when we cannot see what He can do. God's power and divine nature may be invisible to us, but He makes it known to all: "For since the creation of the world God's invisible qualities—his eternal power and divine nature—have been clearly seen, being understood from what has been made" (Rom. 1:20).

God's greatness and power show among the heavens and the earth. God's greatness and power show through the conception of a baby in a mother's womb. God's greatness and power show in men and women who can climb to the top of the tallest mountain. God's greatness and power show in men and women who can travel to the moon. This power that we have comes from inside of us and it has been given to us by God.

We need to understand how we can use this power in our healing journey. There have been times when I have said, "I do not know if I can make it through this." There have been times when I have wanted to give up. There have been times when I have been weak. But when I call on God and remember the power I have through Him, I find my strength: "The Sovereign

LORD is my strength; he makes my feet like the feet of a deer, he enables me to tread on the heights" (Hab. 3:19).

We need to be equipped to fight our battles. *We can* handle this, but we need to "be strong in the Lord and in his mighty power" and we must "put on the full armor of God" (Eph. 6:10-11). The Bible tells us there is evil in this world; there is sin, illness, and pain. But God has a power and greatness beyond the darkness of this world.

Let us read together about the armor of God in Ephesians 6:14–17 and learn how we can put on this armor to help us through our trial. In Ephesians chapter 6, we can stand up against our battle with:

- ➤ Truth (who we are in Christ)
- ➤ Righteousness (finding God's way as the right way)
- ➤ The Gospel of Peace (removing worry and anxiety)
- ➤ Faith (believing the word of God)
- ➤ Salvation (being saved and protected by Christ)
- ➤ The Spirit (word of God)

When we look over this list, we see a commonality among them. These pieces of armor encompass the one and only God Almighty. When we clothe ourselves with Him, then we find this inner strength to be able to overcome everything else around us. We trust that He can help us rise above our illness, trouble, or trial: "The LORD is my strength and my shield; my heart trusts in him, and he helps me" (Ps. 28:7).

When we believe and have faith, God shows us His truth, righteousness, and peace through His word, and we receive the gift of salvation. I am saved through God and I am stronger with God. Every day as I fight, I must ask for God's strength:

"LORD, be gracious to us; we long for you. Be our strength every morning, our salvation in time of distress" (Isa. 33:2).

God has brought me out from the world's distress and my own distress. I have had pain. I have had sadness. I have walked through trials. But God is my Savior, and He saves me from all of it through His power and strength.

God did not leave Jesus alone on the cross to die. Jesus fought until the end, and throughout His life, He carried this full armor of God. Jesus trusted God and shared God's message with everyone He could before He was lifted up into heaven. Before Jesus left this world, He told His disciples to:

> Go into all the world and preach the gospel to all creation. Whoever believes and is baptized will be saved, but whoever does not believe will be condemned. And these signs will accompany those who believe: In my name they will drive out demons; they will speak in new tongues; they will pick up snakes with their hands; and when they drink deadly poison, it will not hurt them at all; they will place their hands on sick people, and they will get well. (Mark 16:15–18)

God's greatness and power allowed the impossible to happen. Through the power of God, He lifted Jesus up from the cross, and Jesus sits at the right hand of God in heaven (Mark 16:19).

The amazing thing is that this power of God continues to be passed from generation to generation. Jesus passed on the armor of God to His disciples and taught them to share this message with everyone. Because they trusted Jesus and God, they went out preaching the gospel and performing miracles themselves. It was through God's greatness and power that they were able to accomplish those things.

Now, through our own faith, we can experience the power of God. Do you believe you can feel it too? I do. I believe God had the power to lift Jesus up to heaven, and I believe God can share His spirit of power with me. Through all the signs and the healing that I have experienced, I share my faith with you and hope God will meet you where you are, to show you His spirit of power too.

Spirit of Self-Discipline

Self-discipline can take on many different meanings, but to help us in our healing journey, we can define it as a way to train our mind, body, and spirit. Think about it: Over the last few weeks of this study we have been growing stronger spiritually and physically. We have been making sure we have time for God through prayer and meditation and for ourselves through rest and clean food for our bodies. We now look to train our bodies more physically and mentally.

If you were to look up *self-discipline* in a dictionary, you may find the meaning to be similar to this one: "The discipline and training of oneself, usually for improvement."[6]

How can we have self-discipline? We look to God. (Have you noticed this pattern in every chapter?) We continue to go to God for everything. We are training our bodies and minds to do this. In Titus 2:11–12, the scripture tells us, "For the grace of God has appeared that offers salvation to all people. It teaches us to say 'No' to ungodliness and worldly passions, and to live self-controlled, upright and godly lives in this present age."

In chapter four when we were saying no to unhealthy foods, we were exhibiting self-control. We naturally wanted to give in to those things. But we are building ourselves up through Christ, and it is through Christ that we are given self-control and self-discipline to overcome worldly pleasures. We will get off track. It can happen and will happen. I remember when I was trying to stay away from sugary treats. I told my husband to hold me accountable, and he did. I did not like it at first because there was this battle inside of me telling me that another piece of cake would taste so good. I felt weak in that moment. If I ate that cake, it would not hurt me, but it would throw me off course. It would derail me from my goal of healing my PCOS symptoms. Having just one more could and would lead me to another and another, and then I would be back to where I had first started.

God gives us His grace and teaches us to say no. God keeps us on course. When I have prayed to God and asked for His help, He has reminded me over and over again what my goal is. He has reminded me of where I am going; He has reminded me of where He wants to take me. And this has motivated me to achieve the goals that He has set before me.

The verses that I am about to share could not have been said more clearly or perfectly. Philippians chapter 3:12–14 says:

> Not that I have already obtained all this, or have already arrived at my goal, but I press on to take hold of that for which Christ Jesus took hold of me. Brothers and sisters, I do not consider myself yet to have taken hold of it. But one thing I do: Forgetting what is behind and straining toward what is ahead, I press on toward the goal to win the prize for which God has called me heavenward in Christ Jesus.

We are all so close to the goal God has set before us. We have taken steps during our journey to find healing. God has pointed out my areas of weakness. Has He pointed out what you struggle with? Let us press on and stick together:

> Join together in following my example, brothers and sisters, and just as you have us as a model, keep your eyes on those who live as we do. For, as I have often told you before and now tell you again even with tears, many live as enemies of the cross of Christ. Their destiny is destruction, their god is their stomach, and their glory is in their shame. Their mind is set on earthly things. But our citizenship is in heaven. And we eagerly await a Savior from there, the Lord Jesus Christ, who, by the power that enables him to bring everything under his control, will transform our lowly bodies so that they will be like his glorious body. (Phil. 3:17–21)

Our prize is in heaven. God is transforming us right in this very moment, and we will be forever transformed when we meet God at His throne. The last verse says that the power of God will transform our lowly bodies so that they will be like His glorious body. God's spirit of power is preparing us for something far greater than we know. He is preparing us for our race.

Think about when you prepare for a race, such as a 5K or half marathon. What do you do to get ready for it? Do you show up that day without any practice? No; of course not. I know if I did I would not be able to put forth my best effort and I would probably be out of breath after the first mile. Scripture tells us:

Everyone who competes in the games goes into strict training. They do it to get a crown that will not last, but we do it to get a crown that will last forever. Therefore I do not run like someone running aimlessly; I do not fight like a boxer beating the air. No, I strike a blow to my body and make it my slave so that after I have preached to others, I myself will not be disqualified for the prize. (1 Cor. 9:25–27)

When we have self-discipline, we train ourselves to prepare for the race or game that is before us. An athlete in training gets up each day and takes steps to push his or her body to get stronger. They are motivated by the prize, trophy, or personal accomplishment. God asks us to "throw off everything that hinders and the sin that so easily entangles. And let us run with perseverance the race marked out for us, fixing our eyes on Jesus, the pioneer and perfecter of faith. For the joy set before him he endured the cross, scorning its shame, and sat down at the right hand of the throne of God" (Heb. 12:1–2).

How can we apply this to our healing process? We have learned through these verses in the chapter to have a spirit of power and a spirit of self-discipline. I need to be strengthened to carry out the works of God. I will not let a disease or a trial slow me down. I look to God and press on toward the goal He has placed in front of me; the gift of salvation is what I race toward. In my time on earth, I want to be strong and allow my body to do what it was meant to do: "Therefore, strengthen your feeble arms and weak knees. 'Make level paths for your feet,' so that the lame may not be disabled, but rather healed" (Heb. 12:12–13).

During my journey, I have found exercise to be very helpful in my healing. It takes my mind off the trial I am going through. When I have been at my weakest, I have chosen a low-impact routine that consists of stretching and walking. When I have felt my best, I have incorporated dance, bike riding, hiking, golf, and cardio workouts into my routine. A simple walk in nature can be so beneficial and eye-opening. It allows you to be out in God's creation listening to the chirping of birds, feeling the warm sunshine, and boosting your energy levels. Two years ago I started a Walking with Jesus group. Women from my small group and church came out and we walked nature trails together. I would pick a verse to talk about and we would pray over any special prayer requests. In this time together, it helped keep my body strong and helped take the focus off the trial I was facing.

When you are choosing an activity to help keep you strong, remember to switch your focus from yourself to God. Ask God to be a part of it. In 1 Timothy 4:8 we are given this advice: "For physical training is of some value, but godliness has value for all things, holding promise for both the present life and the life to come."

We should not feel like we need to hold back. We learn from God that physical training is good for our body and spiritual training is good for our heart. Remember we have been given a spirit of power from God and a spirit of self-discipline that allows us to have control over our bodies and motivate ourselves to try new things. Choose an activity that you will enjoy, and when you do, your heart will be happy.

Spirit of Love

Recently I began taking golf lessons. I have enjoyed golf in the past while playing with my father and sharing this sport with my husband. But I have never really learned the basic techniques of the game. With good rest and more energy, I felt a confidence inside of me to try something new and a power to learn more about this sport.

The evening when I was about to go out for my second lesson, I learned some results of a test I had done. The results were better than the worst-case scenario, but it would mean I would have another bump to overcome in my journey, and I would need a procedure done to correct the issue. When I left for the lesson, I had thoughts running through my mind. I was thankful it was not worse news, but I felt uneasy about it and disappointed. I was sad by the fact that I had been making such good progress in my healing journey and this would throw me off track.

As I learned more about how to chip the ball onto the green and practiced the techniques the instructor taught, my mind and focus were shifted. I was not dwelling on myself and my circumstances, but I was enjoying a simple activity with the gorgeous scenery of the sun setting over the hills. I was among God's creation. I was filling myself up with God's power, self-discipline, and love. I was being strengthened in that moment.

When I left the driving range, I did not feel the same. I had a new perspective on the outcome of those results. I had a choice. I could dwell in my own heart's misery or I could allow the strength of God to fill me up with His love.

For many of us, as we navigate through our trials, we will come across bumps in the road like I did. But we keep focused so we do not lose track of where God wants to take us. We continue to look to God for His strength, His power, and His love. Paul prays this prayer and shares with us how we can be filled by God:

> I pray that out of his glorious riches he may strengthen you with power through his Spirit in your inner being, so that Christ may dwell in your hearts through faith. And I pray that you, being rooted and established in love, may have power, together with all the Lord's holy people, to grasp how wide and long and high and deep is the love of Christ, and to know this love that surpasses knowledge—that you may be filled to the measure of all the fullness of God. (Eph. 3:16–19)

That night, I chose to be filled up by God's power and love. I realized the depth of God's love, and I knew He would give me the strength to help me get over this other obstacle. After having a successful procedure, I was cleared by my doctor, and thankfully I could get back on track and focus on the plans God had for me.

As we gain this sense of strength throughout this chapter, we allow the stem of our plant to grow into a flower bud. If you think about a bud, it stays tightly closed until it has the strength to open. *As we look to God for His strength, we are given a spirit of power.* As His light shines upon us, we are ready to burst open to display our beautiful flower.

For some, one's trial may be coming to an end, one's illness may be close to being in remission, or one may have better control over the struggles they have been facing. Whatever the situation, we now look to God to take one last step and learn how we can open our hearts to a spirit of love. We can learn how we can best love God, ourselves, and others during our trial. We can make changes in our hearts and minds and let God be the strength over our hearts to fully experience the fullness of Him: "My flesh and my heart may fail, but God is the strength of my heart and my portion forever" (Ps. 73:26).

A Prayer to Say to God:

God of strength,
I come to You in my weakness and know You are the God of power. I hope in You, and I pray that I will find a new kind of strength. I ask that You will help me live a self-controlled, godly life. I want to be strengthened by You to carry out the plans You have for me. Thank You for showing me how wide, long, high, and deep Your love is for me, and I hope that I may begin to share my heart openly with others.
Amen.

Week 6: The Power of Seven Challenge

- **Read it, ponder it, and apply it**
- **For the next seven days, focus on finding your strength in God. On each day of the week, open your Bible to *read* the verse listed. Then *ponder* it and answer the daily question. At the end of the week, *apply* what you have learned and come up with a plan to help yourself grow closer to God.**

Day 1

- Read: Psalm 22:19
- Daily Question: What moments have made you feel weak? Did you come to God about them?

Day 2

- Read: Psalm 118:13–14
- Daily Question: Think of your trial or illness as Goliath, the giant. It may seem bigger than you can handle, but then repeat to yourself, "When I am weak, I am strong." We can approach our biggest trials like David did. How can you change your thoughts to be more like David's in facing your own trials?

Day 3

- Read: 1 Corinthians 2:3–5
- Daily Question: In what other ways have you seen God's greatness and power?

Day 4

- Read: Ephesians 6:10–17
- Daily Question: Think about what the full armor of God means to you. How can these words help you during your journey?

Day 5

- Read: 2 Chronicles 15:7
- Daily Question: Have you set a goal before and gotten off track? What happened? What can help you stay more committed to your goal going forward?

Day 6

- Read: Genesis 13:17
- Daily Question: Have you incorporated exercise into your healing journey? What type of movement do you enjoy? What activity could you try outside?

Day 7

- Read: Proverbs 31:17
- Daily Question: How has exercise or an activity helped strengthen you after a bad day? What did you feel or experience?

Apply It: How Can You Grow Closer to God's Light?

1. What small step can you take this week to increase your strength?
   (Ex. Add in a daily walk)

2. What big step can you take over this year to increase your strength?
   (Ex. Try a new activity)

3. How can you carry out your plans?
   (Ex. Ask a friend to join you on your daily walk; look for classes, leagues, or teams in the area and sign up)

7

LOVE

"Create in me a pure heart, O God, and renew
a steadfast spirit within me."

Psalm 51:10

I f someone asked me, "How is your heart doing during this
trial?" what would I say?

As I ponder that question, I think of what that question
means to me.

What is in my heart? What is flowing out of it? Are my
thoughts, words, and actions pleasing to God? Amid the pain
and suffering from my trial, is my heart still filled with the
love of God?

To be honest, very rarely was I checking in with myself and
examining how I was doing through God's eyes, especially
during my trial. I had not looked back over the last several

years, and I really did not want to look back because what I had been walking through was tough and painful.

You see, in addition to the pain and hurt from your trial, you may also be holding on to other past or present pain that is weighing you down. Despite all the progress you have made in your spiritual and physical healing, you may still need to address emotions from your heart.

Ask yourself these three questions as you examine your heart:

1. Am I loving God during my trial?
2. Am I loving myself?
3. Am I being loving towards others?

As you think about your answers to these questions, read Proverbs 4:23: "Above all else, guard your heart, for everything you do flows from it."

For the last seven years since my diagnosis of PCOS, I have been making strides toward a healthier physical and spiritual body. But the one area I was neglecting was my emotional body. A few years ago, I went to a few counseling sessions to discuss what I had been through from the acupuncture experience. I knew I had to work through that pain and through the emotions that had been left unaddressed during my younger years. During the session, the counselor said that we could first set this pain and hurt aside in a box...an invisible box. Then slowly during our sessions we would bring out each topic and work through it. I thought this was a great idea, at least the part where you stuff everything inside the box. I had been doing that all my life: keeping everything inside of me, burying it, hiding it, not addressing it. It was out of sight, out of mind.

But was it really out of my mind? Was it really out of my heart?

In the last chapter, we took a step to allow our plant to grow into a flower bud. There our flower was closed up, waiting for the right opportunity to open up its petals to reveal its beauty. Our flower had two choices: to stay closed up in the darkness of the flower bud or to open up and experience the light of the world.

In the past I did not know how to properly address my emotions. I had been hiding inside this flower bud. I had been choosing to stay inside this darkness. And maybe I was not choosing to be there—no one wants to be there—but I did not know how to open up my petals to experience the light of God and truly find His precious love. When I took a moment to examine my heart, I found I struggled to love myself. I struggled to open up and share my feelings. I struggled with believing I was enough and allowing myself to be vulnerable. I had been hard on myself, and I was trying to live this perfect life that was not achievable. I was missing this step of being open, honest, and real, and in turn, I was not allowing my heart to heal as well.

The greatest lesson I learned as I finished up those counseling sessions was how much God loved me. God loved me for me. I was enough for God. I did not have to be perfect for everyone else. I believed I was valuable to God, and I could now shift my focus to living a life that would please God.

The apostle Paul in 1 Thessalonians urges us to do this: to live a life that will please God by following all the instructions given to us by the authority of the Lord Jesus (1 Thess. 4:1–2). When I learned that lesson, a huge weight was lifted off my shoulders and I could see God's light as clear as day. In my healing journey, I could take this final step. I could allow my plant not only to open up into a beautiful flower but to take it one step further and bear fruit. I wanted my seed to produce more: "But the seed falling on good soil refers to someone who hears the word and understands it. This is the one who produces a crop, yielding a hundred, sixty or thirty times what was sown" (Matt. 13:23).

I knew I was capable of much more. I knew God had much more for me.

When I was touched by Jesus and saw His light, I wanted nothing more than to stay there amongst His light forever. The great news is, we can. God tells us, "For you were once darkness, but now you are light in the Lord. Live as children of light (for the fruit of the light consists in all goodness, righteousness and truth) and find out what pleases the Lord" (Eph. 5:8–10).

We have all been given this calling—to *live as children of light*—and God urges us "to live a life worthy of the calling you have received" (Eph. 4:1).

Now, I do not know about you, but I did not work this hard on my healing not to become the creation God planned for me. Here is our choice: we can comfortably sit exactly where we are, or we can take it a step further by bearing fruit and sharing our journey with others to be an example of joy, hope, and love.

If we are going to live as children of light, we need to know the depth of the love of God, learn to accept it, and imitate it. Before we learn more about loving God, ourselves, and others, let us take a look at the story of Job.

The story of Job allows us to see how God tests His people, how to respond to these tests, and how God's love shines through the pain and suffering. Sometimes it does not make sense to us, and we cannot explain why we are suffering. It may be after the pain that we see how God calls us to His light and uses our lives as a way to teach us and others about His kingdom. I have read over this story many times during my trial, and I can easily relate to Job from experiencing loss to suffering through health challenges. Maybe you can relate too!

In the beginning of the Book of Job, we learn that Job was a good man and had a good life. He was blameless and upright; he feared God and shunned evil (Job 1:1). Job had seven sons and three daughters, and he was considered the greatest man among all the people of the East. The Lord encounters Satan one day and Job's name is mentioned. Satan tells the Lord that Job has been blessed with everything he needs; however, Satan thinks that if you take away the things he has, then Job will no longer be obedient to God. The Lord decides to test Job but tells Satan he cannot do anything to hurt Job. During a short period of time, Job loses his oxen, donkeys, sheep, camels, servants, and all his children to death. Job falls to the ground and says: "Naked I came from my mother's womb, and naked I will depart. The LORD gave and the LORD has taken away; may the name of the LORD be praised" (Job 1:21). Even with losing everything, Job showed his love for God and trusted Him.

Satan returned to God, and Job's name was mentioned again. God tells Satan that Job still remains faithful even despite losing all he had. In Job 2:4–5 it states, "Skin for skin!" Satan replied. "A man will give all he has for his own life. But now stretch out your hand and strike his flesh and bones, and he will surely curse you to your face." The Lord decides to test Job a second time: "The LORD said to Satan, 'Very well, then, he is in your hands; but you must spare his life.' So Satan went out from the presence of the LORD and afflicted Job with painful sores from the soles of his feet to the crown of his head" (Job 2:6–7).

When Job's three friends hear about his suffering, they come to his side to give him comfort for seven days and seven nights. During this week his friends sit quietly by his side. However, Job finally stops the silence and expresses his despair.

Before we learn more about the story, think about how Job's heart might be doing during his trial. Look at what he has been through. He has suffered through losing loved ones, and now he is afflicted with disease. What we start to see come out of his heart is anger and eventually hurtful words. In Job chapter 3, he makes a powerful statement by saying he wishes he was never born. His thinking becomes distorted and he lets his emotions overtake him. In Job 3:26 he states, "I have no peace, no quietness; I have no rest, but only turmoil." Do you think God would be pleased with his words? Would God be pleased with what is in his heart?

I remember this part in my journey, where I felt like I had been through enough. I had carried the pain of losing my mom, the disappointment of my infertility journey, the suffering from PCOS symptoms, and then the ups and downs of our adoption process. During that time, I felt distant from God. I felt drained emotionally, and I remember feeling at my lowest point, similar to how Job was feeling.

In the story Job's friends begin to speak up and give him advice. However, they do not know how to comfort him, and they begin to try to explain why he is suffering. The problem is none of us can truly understand God's ways and why we suffer. Between chapters 4 and 32, Job's friends make strong statements suggesting that he must have committed a sin to be suffering like this. In chapter 12 Job responds to these statements by saying, "I have become a laughingstock to my friends, though I called on God and he answered— a mere laughingstock, though righteous and blameless!" (Job 12:4).

Job thought he was innocent and did not think he had done anything wrong to deserve all of this turmoil. Job's spirit continues to be worn down, and he loses hope. In chapter 21 Job responds to his friends, stating, "So how can you console me with your nonsense? Nothing is left of your answers but falsehood!" (Job 21:34).

In the story Job starts to feel lonely and wonders where God is: "But if I go to the east, he is not there; if I go to the west, I do not find him. When he is at work in the north, I do not see him; when he turns to the south, I catch no glimpse of him" (Job 23:8–9).

During this next moment, Job begins to snap out of his negative thinking and begins to recall his good and loving God. Job says: "But he knows the way that I take; when he has tested me, I will come forth as gold. My feet have closely followed his steps; I have kept to his way without turning aside. I have not departed from the commands of his lips; I have treasured the words of his mouth more than my daily bread" (Job 23:10–12).

During my own tests, I wondered where God was. I felt alone as I walked through these tough moments. And it took a lot of effort to rise above this negative thinking and to come to a place of peace and acceptance of the struggles I was walking through.

Job changes his attitude here and wants to rise above his suffering. Job begins to put his trust back into God and realizes God knows every one of his steps. In chapter 31 Job says we should really let God be the judge, and he attempts to prove his innocence one last time. Job examines his life. He examines his heart. He searches his whole self for any past sin or wrongdoing. And he finds himself to be innocent; at least he thinks he is innocent.

As Job finishes defending himself, another friend—Elihu— speaks up. Elihu also believed that Job was suffering because he did something wrong, but he acknowledges that God is a God of love and can restore Job back to health if he repents.

God finally interrupts all of these arguments and asks Job how he could possibly understand His power and His ability to create the heavens and the earth: "Where were you when I laid the earth's foundation? Tell me, if you understand. Who marked off its dimensions? Surely you know!" (Job 38:4–5).

Over the next four chapters, 38 through 41, God describes in detail all that He is capable of doing, making, and knowing. This finally opens up Job's eyes. And in chapter 42, Job acknowledges his lack of trust and repents to God for the hurt he has caused:

> I know that you can do all things; no purpose of
> yours can be thwarted. You asked, "Who is this
> that obscures my plans without knowledge?"
> Surely I spoke of things I did not understand,
> things too wonderful for me to know. You said,
> "Listen now, and I will speak; I will question
> you, and you shall answer me." My ears had
> heard of you but now my eyes have seen you.
> Therefore I despise myself and repent in dust
> and ashes. (Job 42:2–6)

In the end of the story of Job, God shares how angry He is with his friends and says He will forgive them after Job prays for them. Once Job prays for his friends, the Lord restores Job's health and blesses him with even more than he had before.

Through this story of suffering, forgiveness, and love, we learn if our emotions take hold of us and we believe lies over God's truth, then our thoughts, words, and actions could hurt God, ourselves, and others.

What significance does this story have for us, and what does this story teach us? After reading through this story, the three important points that stood out to me are to:

1. Search my heart during my trial
2. Express my emotions in a way that pleases God
3. Understand God loves me during my trial and He teaches me to love others during their trials

For many of us, we may be like Job—we have been living a good life and then, out of nowhere, we are affected by a big trial such as a disease or an illness. Do you remember what we discussed in chapter one? We learned how God tests us, and we see in this story how Job was tested not just once but twice. Job tried to keep a strong faith during the first test and praised God even after losing the people and animals he loved. But then, after the second test, Job begins to let this trial affect his thoughts and words. His heart grows with darkness and he begins to curse the day he was born.

Now, God does not expect us to hold it all together during our trials, and God openly shows us throughout the Bible that He too is an emotional being. But we need to express our emotions in a way that is pleasing to God. We need to be careful not to sin. Job shows several emotions throughout the book, which include anger, bitterness, sadness, and guilt. And we also see God express His emotion toward Job's three friends: "I am angry with you and your two friends, because you have not spoken the truth about me, as my servant Job has" (Job 42:7).

The one difference to keep in mind between God and us is that He is perfect and does not sin. We can learn from God, and from Jesus, what the best ways are to respond to our suffering without sinning.

So what should we do if we are angry or have feelings that we need to address? In Ephesians 4:26 it says, "In your anger do not sin: Do not let the sun go down while you are still angry, and do not give the devil a foothold."

It is important to express our feelings and talk to God about our pain. In this verse it says that we should not let the sun go down while we are angry. We need to resolve our feelings before they take hold of us. The way I used to handle my emotions was not the right way. By storing them up inside, I was holding on to the darkness of my thoughts. Then if I allowed my negative thoughts to leave my mouth, I was allowing darkness to spread to others. Do you see this vicious cycle that can happen if we are not careful?

To help us live as children of light, Ephesians 5:11 tells us to: "Have nothing to do with the fruitless deeds of darkness, but rather expose them."

We need to expose our feelings and let God show us what is not pleasing in His eyes. God did this with Job. Job could not understand the complexity of God and why he was suffering. Job's anger began to take hold of him and he spoke falsely about God. But God finally stopped him and addressed the charges Job made against Him.

Before we make the same mistakes as Job, we need to search our hearts and see why these feelings are churning within us: "When you are on your beds, search your hearts and be silent" (Ps. 4:4).

If we find things that God may be unpleased with, then we should purge those emotions and "get rid of all bitterness, rage and anger, brawling and slander, along with every form of malice" (Eph. 4:31).

We cannot have darkness within our hearts but be fully in God's light. So before we let bad thoughts take hold of us, we must "take captive every thought to make it obedient to Christ" (2 Cor. 10:5). The thoughts, words, and actions that are obedient to Christ are ones that come from a place of love. Love comes from a pure heart, a good conscience, and a sincere faith. If Job was not so busy being angry and making arguments to prove his innocence, he would have seen that God's love for him was always present. Job thought God was absent during his trial. He said, "I cry out to you, God, but you do not answer; I stand up, but you merely look at me. You turn on me ruthlessly; with the might of your hand you attack me. You snatch me up and drive me before the wind; you toss me about in the storm" (Job 30:20–22).

Do you believe God attacks us? Do you believe He tosses us out in the storm? Is this true or a false teaching that Job believed?

We learn this statement is false. Why? Because in the end of the story, we see that God *does* come to Job's aid to save him from his suffering. It may not be in the timing we want, but He comes when He is ready to. God saves him from the storm, teaches him a lesson, and then shows compassion, mercy, and love to Job by blessing him with more than he had before. In 2 John 1:3 it says, "Grace, mercy, and peace from God the Father and from Jesus Christ, the Father's Son, will be with us in truth and love."

What is the truth?

God does not test us to hurt us but to build us up into holy Christ followers. God chose us to take on this suffering. Job may not have understood why he suffered, and God may not have revealed that to him, but God called him. God had a purpose for his life. God used Job to be an example for us:

"Brothers and sisters, as an example of patience in the face of suffering, take the prophets who spoke in the name of the Lord. As you know, we count as blessed those who have persevered. You have heard of Job's perseverance and have seen what the Lord finally brought about. The Lord is full of compassion and mercy" (James 5:10–11).

We too can persevere through our trial and believe God will show His compassion, mercy, and love to us. So with Paul we join "in suffering for the gospel, by the power of God. He has saved us and called us to a holy life—not because of anything we have done but because of his own purpose and grace" (2 Tim. 1:8–9).

If we say yes to God, we are giving up our life for God's purpose. We are saying yes to God living within us. We are saying yes to living a life of truth. And we are saying yes to living a life of love. So in suffering or not, let us: "Follow God's example, therefore, as dearly loved children and walk in the way of love, just as Christ loved us and gave himself up for us as a fragrant offering and sacrifice to God" (Eph. 5:1–2).

In learning all of this from the story of Job, let us shed whatever darkness is left in us and allow God to dwell in our hearts forever. We want to be amongst God's light. When we are rooted and established in love, we can grasp how wide and long and high and deep the love of Christ is for us (Eph. 3:17–18). While suffering or not, may we not forget this truth of God.

In the final section of this chapter and of this book, we learn what God's love is and how to accept it into our own lives and share it with others. It is important to note that love is the first fruit of the Spirit mentioned. God demonstrates His love for us all across the Bible, and if we do not truly know what love means, we can not apply it to our own lives and share it with the lives of others.

In 1 Corinthians 13 we learn the definition of love. Can you recall where this scripture has been used before? Maybe at a wedding ceremony? My husband and I picked these verses during our ceremony, but as we look at it now, let us discover a far deeper meaning. A meaning that will help us understand what God's love encompasses, not just in marriages but all throughout our lives.

In 1 Corinthians 13:4–7 says, "Love is patient, love is kind. It does not envy, it does not boast, it is not proud. It does not dishonor others, it is not self-seeking, it is not easily angered, it keeps no record of wrongs. Love does not delight in evil but rejoices with the truth. It always protects, always trusts, always hopes, always perseveres."

What is love?	What is it not?
Patient	Envious
Kind	Boastful
Joyful	Proud
Protective	Dishonoring
Trusting	Selfish
Hopeful	Angry
Persevering	Evil

If we are going to be imitators of God, then we need to be following the list on the left side. Every day we need to be actively checking our hearts to follow the ways of God. If you continue acting in ways that are not loving, then think about what impact that may have on your own suffering. As we learn more about God's love, we will learn how to apply this to our own lives as we conclude the final step in our healing journey.

God's Love

God's love for us is clear starting from the beginning of creation, and we have learned that our troubles and hardships will not stand between the love God has for us: "For I am convinced that neither death nor life, neither angels nor demons, neither the present nor the future, nor any powers, neither height nor depth, nor anything else in all creation, will be able to separate us from the love of God that is in Christ Jesus our Lord" (Rom. 8:38–39).

God is for us, and He shows His goodness to us. God sent down His blessings upon the earth for all of us to enjoy. Recall the story of Noah, which we discussed in chapter one. In the story Noah shows us how we should live our lives: righteous, blameless, and walking faithfully with God (Gen. 6:9). We also see how much God loved Noah and Noah loved God in return.

Noah simply followed all the commands God asked him to, and by doing this, God gave us a promise. God's promise is a covenant that allows us to remember His connection with us:

> And God said, "This is the sign of the covenant I am making between me and you and every living creature with you, a covenant for all generations to come: I have set my rainbow in the clouds, and it will be the sign of the covenant between me and the earth. Whenever I bring clouds over the earth and the rainbow appears in the clouds, I will remember my covenant between me and you and all living creatures

of every kind. Never again will the waters become a flood to destroy all life. Whenever the rainbow appears in the clouds, I will see it and remember the everlasting covenant between God and all living creatures of every kind on the earth" (Gen. 9:12–16).

Do you know that the morning after I had my encounter with Jesus, I saw a rainbow in the clear morning sky? During my walk that morning, I was thinking about God and how much He had blessed me. As soon as I came around the corner of our neighborhood, I saw a rainbow and I recalled these verses. God's love surrounded me, and His covenant will always remind me of His unfailing *love*: "Know therefore that the LORD your God is God; he is the faithful God, keeping his covenant of love to a thousand generations of those who love him and keep his commandments" (Deut. 7:9).

God's covenant is not the only thing that He gave for those He loves. God took it one step further to take death out of the world, and He devised a plan to remove darkness from our lives. God's love for us cannot be made more visible than Him sending His one and only Son to die for our sins: "You see, at just the right time, when we were still power-less, Christ died for the ungodly. Very rarely will anyone die for a righteous person, though for a good person someone might possibly dare to die. But God demonstrates his own love for us in this: While we were still sinners, Christ died for us" (Rom. 5:6–8).

From childhood our hearts have been inclined to evil (Gen. 8:21). They have been inclined to be envious, boastful, proud, dishonoring, selfish, and angry.

When I was five years old, I saw how this could be true. My parents signed me up for soccer. It was a coed team, and unlike several other kids on the team, I had never played before. During the first practice, I was laughed at for not knowing how to dribble the soccer ball up to the cone and back. My heart was crushed. During the middle of practice, I ran over to my parents crying, and I chose not to return to the team. My days of soccer ended in one practice. The words and actions of these children affected my confidence and crushed my self-worth. I not only heard these hurtful words then, but all throughout middle school, high school, and college, I noticed how words and actions affected the lives of others.

Thankfully *God's love is bigger than hurtful words and judgments.* For some, you may have had to deal with a similar situation or multiple situations all your life. God's love for each of us shows us *our self-worth comes from Him and Him alone*: "Blessed is the one who trusts in the LORD, whose confidence is in him. They will be like a tree planted by the water that sends out its roots by the stream. It does not fear when heat comes; its leaves are always green. It has no worries in a year of drought and never fails to bear fruit" (Jer. 17:7–8).

By trusting in God and having this confidence in Him, we can stand up to any sinful attacks that come our way. We can stay true to who we are and continue to carry out the plans that God has for us.

Love God

When we accepted God into our lives and into our hearts, we said no—and continue to say no—to the sinful nature that tries to overtake our lives, and we said *yes* to the Spirit of God: "Therefore, brothers and sisters, we have an obligation—but it is not to the flesh, to live according to it. For if you live according to the flesh, you will die; but if by the Spirit you put to death the misdeeds of the body, you will live. For those who are led by the Spirit of God are the children of God" (Rom. 8:12–14).

If we were born in sin and are tempted by sin, how do we break this cycle so our hearts may heal?

God offers us the chance to break free from our sinful heart: "My son, do not forget my teaching, but keep my commands in your heart, for they will prolong your life many years and bring you peace and prosperity. Let love and faithfulness never leave you; bind them around your neck, write them on the tablet of your heart. Then you will win favor and a good name in the sight of God and man" (Prov. 3:1–4).

The most important command we can follow is to love God. Through God's love, we are taught to love: "We love because he first loved us" (1 John 4:19). When we love God, this love is passed down to us so we may love ourselves and share love with others. Our heart follows in step with God, and we keep these commands in the center of our hearts. Then we can live by the fruit of the Spirit by having: "love, joy, peace, forbearance, kindness, goodness, faithfulness, gentleness and self-control" (Gal. 5:22).

Love Yourself

If our desire has been to follow the commands of God, why is it still hard to love ourselves and others?

Think about this question: *What if Jesus asked you if He could wash your feet?*

My first response when I read the passage of John 13 was, *How could I let Jesus do that? Do I deserve His love?*

This is God's true test to see where our hearts are:

1. Will you follow His command? Will you obey? Will you trust Him?
2. Will you allow Him to see who you are? The good and the bad?
3. Will you humble yourself before Him?

If you are ignoring His commands, then are you not accepting His love? A trial like the one I have faced has given me a new perspective. It has allowed me to examine my life. It has helped me to see what is in my heart and allows me to be cleansed of any unrighteousness.

The Bible reminds us that our days are short: "Our days may come to seventy years, or eighty, if our strength endures; yet the best of them are but trouble and sorrow, for they quickly pass, and we fly away" (Ps. 90:10).

I don't want to wait. The day will come when I stand before God, and I want Him to find good favor in me like He did with Noah.

If given the choice to accept Jesus's act of kindness by cleansing my feet, I would be silly not to say yes.

I want to be living righteously now during my trial and continue to live a righteous life after my trial is over. My healing journey could not be complete if I continued to be hard on myself, if I was blaming myself for past mistakes, or if I was still holding on to guilt in my heart. During my suffering, God led me to this passage: "LORD, do not rebuke me in your anger or discipline me in your wrath. Your arrows have pierced me, and your hand has come down on me. Because of your wrath there is no health in my body; there is no soundness in my bones because of my sin. My guilt has overwhelmed me like a burden too heavy to bear" (Ps. 38:1–4).

I had always considered myself a good person, but when I read this verse, I saw flashes of past mistakes that had hurt myself and hurt others. I had to make them right.

So I took some time to examine my heart. I reviewed the words from 1 Corinthians 13:4–7 and sat and thought about if I had been envious, boastful, proud, rude, selfish, angry, or evil.

And to be honest, when I did this exercise for myself, the area that I struggled with was envy. When I was younger, I knew God loved me, but I did not understand the extent of His love. I was not able to see all that I had, because my focus was distracted by the talent, achievements, and success of others around me. Envy and jealousy came up again in my heart when my husband and I struggled with infertility. It was hard to see so many around us be blessed with children when we struggled to grow our family.

But my perspective changed when I opened up to God about these feelings and examined them. I was no longer allowing them to stay buried in my heart. And when I brought them to light, I was able to let go of them. I was able to replace my old heart with a new loving heart. A heart that is patient, joyful, kind, protective, trusting, hopeful, and perservering.

After acknowledging what situations were still in my heart, I chose to make them right. For me to move on from them, I addressed them and repented for them. With a healed heart, I was able to show love to myself and to others. You see, when you learn the wisdom of God by following His commands, you'll understand how to walk righteously with God: "The one who gets wisdom loves life; the one who cherishes understanding will soon prosper" (Prov. 19:8).

When we love ourselves for who we are—who God made us to be—we find our value and worth from God.

Regularly allowing ourselves to be cleansed from our emotions and sins helps us to release them from our body. God is watching to see if you will obey Him and allow Him to help you grow through your suffering. Remember in 2 Kings 5, where Naaman was told to wash himself seven times in the Jordan and his skin would be cured from leprosy. Naaman had pride in his heart and refused at first. But once he addressed those feelings and made it right, God restored him. Naaman was cleansed of his pride and cleansed of his disease.

As you move forward, do not let the world control your hearts, because the world will cause you to focus on the sinful nature and you'll be left feeling empty. Instead continue to move forward with the truth of God etched on your heart and focus on how full your heart of love is.

We can appreciate our existence and walk humbly next to God. Our eyes are opened to see His love. Our hearts are opened to accept His love. And our hearts begin to be opened to share His love.

Love Others

After Jesus was finished with washing the feet of His disciples in John 13, He asked if they understood what He had done for them: "You call me 'Teacher' and 'Lord,' and rightly so, for that is what I am. Now that I, your Lord and Teacher, have washed your feet, you also should wash one another's feet. I have set you an example that you should do as I have done for you" (John 13:13–15).

What is Jesus telling us in these verses? Jesus has shown us His love by cleansing us from our sins, and we are now called to share the love of God with others.

I believe my trial has been a way for God to bring me to the calling that He has set before me. When I started suffering, I did not know God would teach me about these seven steps of healing. I did not know He would give me the wisdom to fulfill this calling by writing this book. And I certainly did not expect that He would give me the strength to tear down my walls and open up my life for all to see.

God uses us through our trials to be an example to others. God has used so many in the Bible to teach us His lessons. Think about Noah one last time. Noah was given a calling to build an ark. But Noah was a farmer, "a man of the soil" (Gen. 9:20). He was not a carpenter, but God gave him the instructions to build an ark, the wisdom to fulfill this calling, and the strength to carry it out. Noah followed every one of the steps God gave him and fulfilled the purpose he was called to.

In high school I had made plans and set goals for my life. Goals to one day be a nurse, get married, and have several children. Some of these plans happened as God wanted them to be and some did not, but I believe the greatest one that He has led me to be is His servant and to share my gifts with others. On the night of my encounter with Jesus, I felt a prompting to share my healing journey with the world.

If you look back at the life of Paul, you see God gave him a purpose to carry out the message of Christ and to share the love of God with others. In Ephesians 3:7 Paul writes from prison and says, "I became a servant of this gospel by the gift of God's grace given me through the working of his power."

Our suffering should not push us apart, but it should bring us closer together. We find others who have walked through the same kind of suffering or trials, and we open our own lives to help each other. My suffering from infertility and PCOS may help another person persevere and find healing.

A person in remission from cancer may help another person with cancer walk through the painful treatments and hospitalizations that they may encounter. We unite in the body of Christ, and follow the words of Paul:

> Be completely humble and gentle; be patient, bearing with one another in love. Make every effort to keep the unity of the Spirit through the bond of peace. There is one body and one Spirit, just as you were called to one hope when you were called; one Lord, one faith, one baptism; one God and Father of all, who is over all and through all and in all. But to each one of us grace has been given as Christ apportioned it. This is why it says: "When he ascended on high, he took many captives and gave gifts to his people." (Eph. 4:2–7)

Through God's love and grace, He has called each of us by name and blessed us with gifts. These gifts help carry out His plans and spread love throughout the world. What gifts have you been given?

Romans 12:6–8 helps us to think about the different spiritual gifts God has blessed us with. Which one of these gifts can you begin to use to help build up the kingdom of God?

"If your gift is prophesying, then prophesy in accordance with your faith; if it is serving, then serve; if it is teaching, then teach; if it is to encourage, then give encouragement; if it is giving, then give generously; if it is to lead, do it diligently; if it is to show mercy, do it cheerfully."

We live our lives for the will of God and begin to use these gifts as we mature and grow. The person I was when I was first diagnosed is not the same person I am today. Through every one of my tests and trials, I stand here for God, asking Him to reveal His will over my life.

I have established my roots in a strong foundation of faith and have built my life up to share God's love: "Speaking the truth in love, we will grow to become in every respect the mature body of him who is the head, that is, Christ. From him the whole body, joined and held together by every supporting ligament, grows and builds itself up in love, as each part does its work" (Eph. 4:15–16).

If we can all follow His commands and build up His kingdom, we will remain in His love forever and we will find that His joy may be in us and our joy may be complete (John 15:9–11). *When I love God...when I love myself...when I love others...I find this pure joy that has been given to me through God the Father.*

I rejoice in God, who is greater than all my circumstances. He is greater than all my trials. He is greater than all my suffering. I rise because I have God to lift me up. On each new day, all I need to do is look up and see His light shining ever brighter over me.

Even after my diagnosis of PCOS, infertility, and other health challenges, I have seen my greater purpose. I have seen how I can persevere through tough times, and I will continue to show my love for God by praising His name:

> Praise be to the God and Father of our Lord Jesus Christ! In his great mercy he has given us new birth into a living hope through the resurrection of Jesus Christ from the dead, and into an inheritance that can never perish, spoil, or fade. This inheritance is kept in heaven for you, who through faith are shielded by God's power

until the coming of the salvation that is ready to be revealed in the last time. In all this you greatly rejoice, though now for a little while you may have had to suffer grief in all kinds of trials. These have come so that the proven genuineness of your faith—of greater worth than gold, which perishes even though refined by fire—may result in praise, glory and honor when Jesus Christ is revealed. Though you have not seen him, you love him; and even though you do not see him now, you believe in him and are filled with an inexpressible and glorious joy, for you are receiving the end result of your faith, the salvation of your souls. (1 Pet. 1:3–9)

As I rejoice in my sufferings and share the transformation I found amongst His light, I hope you can also see the place where you started and the place where you are now. You first placed your seed in God's good soil and took a step of faith, not knowing where God might take you or knowing how He might change you. You allowed your roots to grow in Him and you let God lift you up to His light. May you now clearly see the love He shares with you and feel an inexpressible and glorious joy that you too were called to be a *child of light.*

Your Prayer to God:

In the last chapters, I provided prayers to use. This time I will let you open up to God and share what is in your heart. Use verses from this chapter or the message to create a prayer to God. May the Holy Spirit guide you in your words and allow you to open up and be vulnerable with God as you show Him how much you love Him.

Week 7: The Power of Seven Challenge

- **Read it, ponder it, and apply it**
- **For the next seven days, focus on finding God's love. On each day of the week, open your Bible to *read* the verse listed. Then *ponder* it and answer the daily question. At the end of the week, *apply* what you have learned and come up with a plan to help yourself grow closer to God.**

Day 1

- Read: Psalm 73:21–26
- Daily Question: How has your heart been doing during your trial? Have you left emotions unaddressed?

Day 2

- Read: 1 John 2:3–10
- Daily Question: Have you been showing God your love for Him by obeying His commands? How can you live as a *child of light?*

Day 3

- Read: Job 16:6–12
- Daily Question: Have you experienced feelings like Job? Have you handled them in a way that would be pleasing to God?

Day 4

- Read: Job 42:10–17
- Daily Question: What can you learn from the story of Job? Do you have a new perspective of your suffering?

Day 5

- Read: Colossians 3:12–17
- Daily Question: Look at this heart and take a minute to examine your heart right now. Do you have anything holding you back from stepping fully into God's light? Read each word, and then ask yourself, *Have I been envious, boastful, proud, dishonoring, selfish, angry, or evil?* Circle the words that you feel convicted by. Write off to the side any situations or events that you need to address and that are still coming to your mind. What can you do to make them right with God?

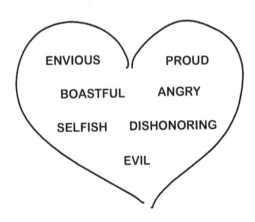

Day 6

- Read: Philippians 2:1–11
- Daily Question: How can you be a servant of God? How can your gifts help others?

Day 7

- Read: 1 Peter 2:21–25
- Daily Question: Do you have a calling from God that He has asked you to carry out? Is your purpose now clear to you?

Apply It: How Can You Grow Closer to God's Light?

1. What small step can you take this week to imitate God's love?
   (Ex. Show love to a friend or family member)

2. What big step can you take over this year to imitate God's love?
   (Ex. Think of what gifts you have been given and begin to share them with others)

3. How can you carry out your plans?
   (Ex. Drop flowers off for your friend or family member; Volunteer at your church and share your gifts)

CONCLUSION

Picture day!

For any thirteen-year-old girl, her makeup, hairstyle, and outfit would need to be simply perfect. But those things seemed trivial on this late September morning.

My mom was sick. My mom was weak. My mom could no longer climb the stairs up to her bedroom to sleep. So as I came downstairs to greet her good morning, I found her lying on the couch, repeating the words "Lift me up."

In that moment, all I could think about was helping her. So I proceeded to lift her up and reposition her until she was comfortable. As my time before school started to slowly dwindle away, I quickly changed into my outfit and stopped one last time to say good-bye to her. I gave her a kiss on the top of her forehead and headed out the door to catch the bus.

This September morning in 1997 was the same day my dad picked me up early from school. It was the day God called my mom to heaven.

The words "Lift me up" have resonated with me since that late September morning. And through my own suffering, I have felt God lift me up above my troubles, above my pain, above the trials I have faced, and He has brought me to His light. He has shown me how beautiful His light is.

As I look back over my mom's life and think of the lessons God has taught me through my suffering, I realize I had already started to observe these steps in my younger years. My mom had a strong foundation of faith; prayed often; meditated on God's word; nourished her body with healthy food; rested; gained strength; and loved God, herself, and others greatly.

Although this was not an easy childhood, it is a part of my story and my journey up until this point. The trials I have endured and suffered have made me the person God needs me to be for His kingdom. God has used all of these hardships for His greater good, and through them I have grown into the creation He wants me to be. I have been transformed into a servant for the Lord God Almighty sharing the gospel with others.

Today my symptoms of PCOS have diminished, and I have a sense of peace over my infertility. God may have other plans for our family that I do not know of yet, but I am able to wait patiently for His plans to be revealed. I look up to Him and I feel a sense of joy with where my life is. As I take these lessons with me, I find more. I find more of God's goodness.

After building upon a foundation of faith with prayer, meditation, nourishment, rest, strength, and love, I find God's sweet treasures. At the end of each chapter, you may have already started to see what God shares with us, but this is what I have found through my suffering.

- ➢ In laying my foundation of faith, I found hope.
- ➢ In praying often, I found patience.
- ➢ In meditating on God's word, I found truth.
- ➢ In nourishing my body with God's food and water, I found contentment.
- ➢ In allowing my body to rest, I found peace.

> ➤ In gaining strength through God, I found power.
> ➤ In loving God, myself, and others, I found *joy*.

Think about this for a moment: If we were that seed in the beginning of chapter one, we at first did not know if we would be able to survive the storm. The wind could have pushed us away from God. The rain could have flooded the ground, not giving us a chance to establish our roots. And the thunder and lightning could have scared us away. But that was not God's plan. God allowed us to sprout our roots in Him and has helped us grow into the creation He needs us to be. As we come out stronger from our own trial, we remain in Him. Our seed stands on good soil with a noble and good heart, hearing the word, retaining it, and we persevere!

Lastly, as I recall the strawberry plant my seven-year-old daughter and I planted in our neighborhood garden, I remember noticing this young plant maturing and bearing much fruit. I could not help but feel that this plant was similar to me and my journey. This plant not only bloomed with beautiful white flowers but produced vines or "runners" with strawberries. It took time to grow and mature, and it needed to be well-tended to. As I was the gardener to this plant, God has been my gardener throughout this journey and will continue to be with me: "I am the true vine, and my Father is the gardener. He cuts off every branch in me that bears no fruit, while every branch that does bear fruit he prunes so that it will be even more fruitful. You are already clean because of the word I have spoken to you. Remain in me, as I also remain in you. No branch can bear fruit by itself; it must remain in the vine. Neither can you bear fruit unless you remain in me" (John 15:1–4).

Going forward, God will cut off the branches that bear no fruit in me and He will prune the ones which will become more fruitful. I remain in Him and He remains in me. When I accepted Jesus as my personal Lord and Savior and God as my Father, I put my trust in Them. No matter what circumstance, trial, or suffering I may walk through in the future, I will continue to live a life that is pleasing to God by: "Bearing fruit in every good work, growing in the knowledge of God, being strengthened with all power according to his glorious might so that you [I] may have great endurance and patience, and giving joyful thanks to the Father, who has qualified you [me] to share in the inheritance of his holy people in the kingdom of light" (Col. 1:10–12).

My heart is full of His goodness and I will continue to sing of His love for all His people:

> My heart, O God, is steadfast,
> my heart is steadfast;
> I will sing and make music.
> Awake, my soul!
> Awake, harp and lyre!
> I will awaken the dawn.
> I will praise you, Lord, among the nations;
> I will sing of you among the peoples.
> For great is your love, reaching to the heavens;
> your faithfulness reaches to the skies.
> Be exalted, O God, above the heavens;
> LET YOUR GLORY BE OVER ALL THE EARTH.
> (Ps. 57:7–11)

ENDNOTES

Chapter 1:

1   Kari Jobe. *I Am Not Alone*, by Jeremy Edwardson, Kari Jobe, Christopher York, and Jimmy James, compact disc, track 9 on Majestic, Sparrow Records, 2014.

Chapter 4:

2   Jonathan Hewett, "Water in the Bible," Learn the Bible, accessed November 28, 2020, http://www.learnthebible. org/water-in-the-bible.html.

3   Jillian Levy, "Broccoli Nutrition: Battle Cancer, Osteoporosis and Weight Gain," Dr. Axe, July 23, 2019, https://draxe. com/nutrition/broccoli-nutrition/.

4   "What Are Clean and Unclean Foods," Bible Study, last modified August 16, 2020, https://www.biblestudy.org/ cleanfood.html.

5   Rachael Link, "Egg Nutrition and Health Benefits Explain Why It's A Superior Food," Dr. Axe, October 21, 2019, https://draxe.com/nutrition/health-benefits-of-eggs/.

Chapter 6:

6   Dictionary.com, s.v. "self-discipline," accessed November 29, 2020, https://www.dictionary.com/browse/self-discipline.

AUTHOR

Arianne Finan was born and raised in the Midwest. In college she met her husband, Jim. They have been married for twelve years. Jim and Arianne have a beautiful daughter. In 2015, they moved to Texas, and during a period of five years, Arianne learned these seven lessons of healing and finished the chapters for her book.

Her family has a passion for helping animals and they had the opportunity to care for over ten pugs from the DFW Pug Rescue group. Their family now includes six furry pets: two dogs and four cats.

Arianne has earned a bachelor's degree in psychology and an associate degree in health information management. She has been frequently involved in her church's ministry programs, including children's ministry. Arianne looks forward to seeing where God takes her next and working alongside her daughter to create a children's book.

To learn more about Arianne, and to find additional
resources, visit ariannefinan.com

If you would like to share your story with Arianne,
write to her at,
arianne@ariannefinan.com

She looks forward to hearing from you.

CPSIA information can be obtained
at www.ICGtesting.com
Printed in the USA
LVHW041329150621
690265LV00005B/61

9 781662 808289